New forms of work organisation

Lisl Klein

*Tavistock Institute
of Human Relations*

Cambridge University Press

Cambridge
London · New York · Melbourne

Published by the Syndics of the Cambridge University Press
The Pitt Building, Trumpington Street, Cambridge CB2 1RP
Bentley House, 200 Euston Road London NW1 2DB
32 East 57th Street, New York, NY 10022, USA
296 Beaconsfield Parade, Middle Park, Melbourne 3206, Australia

First published 1976

Printed in Great Britain by
W & J Mackay Limited, Chatham

Library of Congress Cataloguing in Publication Data
Klein, Lisl.
    New forms of work organisation.
    Bibliography: p.
    1. Work design. 1. Title.
T60.8.K59   658.5'3   75-22556
ISBN 0 521 21055 0

Thanks are due to A. Wilkinson for permission to quote from *A
Survey of Some Western European Experiments in Motivation*; and to the
publishers for the following: Fondazione Giulio Pastore (Rome),
for J. I. Karlsen's 'A Monograph on the Norwegian Industrial
Democracy Project'; the Tavistock Institute of Human Relations
(London), for A. K. Rice's *Productivity and Social Organization*; the
Controller of Her Majesty's Stationery Office (London), for N. A.
B. Wilson's 'On the Quality of Working Life'; Ergon Press (Cork),
for F. E. Emery's 'The Democratisation of the Workplace'; and
Appleton-Century-Crofts, Inc. (New York), for R. F. Hoxie's
Scientific Management and Labor.

Contents

Preface and acknowledgements   *page* vii

1 **The importance of work organisation**   1
  Consequences for individuals   1
  Consequences for culture   6

2 **Assumptions, values, and responses in work
  organisation**   14
  Rationalised production   14
  Responses to rationalised production   16

3 **New thinking in work organisation**   24
  Exercising organisational choice – A case study   24
  A new frame of reference – Industrial democracy   29
  New criteria   36
  New methods   39

4 **Current developments in work organisation**   43
  The development of experiments and programmes   43
  Developments in Sweden   44
  Results of experiments and programmes   46

5 **Discussion – The next generation of issues**   70
  Work design in context   70
  Issues of theory and method   76
  Policy-making as a learning process   85

Appendix 1. Extracts from *Scientific Management and Labor*
  by R. F. Hoxie   88
Appendix 2. Some policy suggestions   101
References   103

Preface and acknowledgements

The Kommission für wirtschaftlichen und sozialen Wandel (Commission for Economic and Social Change) was set up in the Federal Republic of Germany by Chancellor Willy Brandt in 1971. Its task was defined as helping the government towards an informed social policy: on the basis of existing knowledge and commissioned research, it was to advise the government on action in the field of social, economic, and educational policy to facilitate the processes of technical and social change in such a way that they would serve the interests of the community.

In 1972 the Commission invited me to review the present situation in relation to the design of jobs and the organisation of work. They asked for two things: a state-of-the-art report on theories and methods in the field of work organisation, and a critical commentary on some of the developments in this field which are now going on in Europe, with some views on the new problems which they reveal. This monograph, which has already been published in Germany, is the result.

The project provided a welcome opportunity to clarify my own thinking and experience on the subject, and to add to them by reading, talking with experts, visiting a number of institutions around Europe, and renewing contact with a number of old friends and colleagues, and meeting new ones.

In the course of the project I have paid brief visits to Holland, Norway, and Sweden and talked with a number of people in the U.K., as well as with some American visitors who were passing through. The time available was short, and the coverage has not been systematic or comprehensive, either in terms of countries visited or in terms of institutions.

The most obvious omission is Germany itself. I was not familiar with the German scene at the time and the Commission agreed that it would be best, in the time available, not even to try to cover it.

So, while I blush when I think of the people and institutions I did not visit, I would like to express my thanks to the following: Mr D. Wallis, Mr G. C. White, Miss M. Towy-Evans (Department of Employment, London); Professor B. Shackel, Professor A. B. Cherns (University of Technology, Loughborough); Dr G. W. Higgin, Dr E. J. Miller, Dr H. Murray (Tavistock Institute of Human Relations); Professor E. N. Corlett (University of Birmingham); Dr N. A. B. Wilson; Professor L. E. Davis (University of California, Los Angeles); Professor E. L. Trist (Wharton School, University of Pennsylvania); Professor H. J. J. van Beinum (Foundation for Business Administration, Rotterdam); Mr J. R. de Jong (Berenschot, Management Consultants, Utrecht); Professor E. Thorsrud, Dr P. G. Herbst, Dr T. Qvale (Work Research Institutes, Oslo); Mr Lars Ødegaard (Norwegian Employers' Confederation); Mr Reine Hansson, Professor M. Hedberg (Swedish Council for Personnel Administration); Mr R. Lindholm, Mr J.-P. Norstedt (Swedish Employers' Confederation); Mr I. Janérius (Swedish Trade Union Congress (LO)); Mr J. Ulsson (Swedish Metalworkers' Trade Union); Mr F. Ström (Delegationen för förvaltningsdemokrati, Stockholm); Mr O. Hammarström (Industridepartementet, Företagsdemokratidelegationen, Stockholm); Mr I. Erixon (Statsföretag AB, Stockholm); Dr U. Åberg, Dr S.-Å. Johansson (Royal Institute of Technology, Stockholm); Dr B. Stymne (School of Business Administration and Economics, Stockholm).

Also, members of the staff of Koninklijke Nederlandse Hoogovens en Staalfabrieken N.C., Ijmuiden; N.V. Philips' Gloeilampenfabrieken, Eindhoven; AB Orrefors Glasbruk, Orrefors; Philips Electronic & Associated Industries Ltd, London.

December 1975   L.K.

1. The importance of work organisation

Issues of human welfare can be ranged along a continuum from those most internal to the individual – concerned with his most personal needs and development in life – to those which are external to him – concerned with political and social organisation in the world around him. The way in which work is organised has relevance at many points on this continuum.

At the individual, personal level, work is a main means of achieving economic viability and adult status in the Western world, of expressing and developing the personality, and of relating to society. At an intermediate level, the way in which people spend their working lives – that is most of their waking lives – helps to shape their perceptions and attitudes and therefore in turn has cultural and social consequences. At the level of the wider society, the forms taken by the division of labour have led to structural and class alignments, to the creation of political 'worker' or 'labour' parties in a number of European countries, and to the development of trade union movements with varying degrees of political as well as economic power. In the future, it is likely to become the subject of international politics as well, firstly because of the development of multinational employers, and secondly because, in a variety of ways, the more prosperous nations are exporting some of their tasks to the less prosperous nations.

At any one of these levels enough is known now to tackle the problems, if not entirely to solve them. Some of the most important questions, therefore, now arise from the difficulty of relating the different levels to each other, since solutions at one level can conflict with solutions at another.

Consequences for individuals

To begin, then, with the individual. Psychoanalysts do not all take the same view about whether the importance of work in human life has direct biological origins or derived cultural ones. Some attribute it to a primary biological drive to master the environment; others to a more socio-cultural force, the pleasure which is gained from achievement. This includes both the achievement of the immediate and direct consequences of performing a task, and the achievement of independence, freedom, and security(37).*

Whatever the answer to this dilemma, i.e. whatever the basic origins of the importance of work, Freud saw the function of work as providing one of man's main links with reality:

Laying a stress upon importance of work has a greater effect than any other technique of living in the direction of binding the individual more closely to reality; in his work he is at least securely attached to a part of reality, the human community. Work is no less valuable for the opportunity it and the human relations connected with it provide for a very considerable charge of libidinal component impulses, . . . than because it is indispensable for subsistence and justifies existence in a society. The daily work of earning a livelihood affords particular satisfaction when it has been selected by free choice, i.e. when through sublimation it enables use to be made of the existing inclinations, of instinctual impulses that have retained their strength, or are more intense than usual for constitutional reasons(16).

This view is substantiated by studies of the unemployed and by the problems experienced by people after retirement. The nature of the link with reality is discussed by Jahoda(25), who suggests a number of dimensions: first, work strengthens the experience of the passing of time, people without work tending to lose a sense of time; second, work 'encourages the continuous action necessary to maintain objective knowledge of reality', since the ordinary man needs to experience the consequences of his actions and to put his subjective knowledge of reality continuously to the test; third, work permits the pleasurable experience of competence; fourth, work adds to the individual's store of conventional knowledge, particularly his knowledge of inter-dependence with others in common purposes; fifth, work permits the enrichment of the world of immediate experience, and it permits the mutual re-

* References, cited by numbers in round brackets, are listed on pp. 103–6.

inforcement of pleasure and reality principles as regulators of adult behaviour.

Among the scenarios for the future which are currently being discussed is one which predicts the disappearance of work. This not only seems rather unrealistic, but it also raises the prospect of immense personal, and therefore social, difficulties. The transition to an absence of work would be, at the very least, extremely difficult to make and would produce many casualties. If scarcity is no longer the dominant driving force and there is spare capacity(22), it would seem better to devote this capacity to modifying work so that it in fact has more of the characteristics which are helpful to men in their development.

Among social as distinct from clinical researchers, there now exists a very large body of research about work satisfaction among various kinds of working populations, generally expressed in such statistics as labour turnover or absence rates, or in responses to interviews or questionnaires. One recent contribution by Frederick Herzberg(21) makes the distinction between extrinsic or 'hygiene' factors in the work situation, and intrinsic or 'motivating' factors. Faced with conflicting evidence from the literature on the subject, the research workers asked their respondents to describe times when they had been particularly happy in their work situation and times when they had been particularly unhappy. A large number of these incidents were collected and analysed, and the following pattern emerged from the analysis:

When people talked of times when they were dissatisfied, the reasons fell into these groups:

> company policy and administration,
> supervision (technical),
> salary,
> interpersonal relations (supervisory), and
> working conditions.

On the other hand, when people talked of times when they had been happy, the reasons fell into different groups. These were:

> achievement,
> recognition for achievement,
> the work itself, and
> responsibility.

3

The first time this enquiry was made was among a group of middle-management people, accountants and engineers. It has since been repeated among a variety of jobs, at many levels, and in a number of different countries, and the main findings still hold good.

The important thing about these findings is that the two lists are different. They represent not opposite ends of the same scale, but different scales. The things that lead to positive satisfaction and the things that cause dissatisfaction are different in kind, and not merely different in the way people feel about them. This explains a good deal of management (and perhaps government) heartache: it means that however much is done to remove grievances or to improve working conditions in any particular situation, nothing has necessarily been done thereby to create positive satisfaction. At best the result will be what has been called a mood of 'dull contentment'. It also means that in any situation both questions need to be asked. (It must be remembered, incidentally, that an important function of money is as a symbol of achievement and recognition for achievement.)

However, social researchers also have their disagreements. There is a good deal of consensus about what characteristics of jobs people like or dislike, but some disagreement about whether all populations exhibit these needs to the same degree, given that their experiences outside the work situation vary – in other words, about how far it is possible to generalise about human needs in work. One group of researchers has found differences between sub-cultures, specifically between workers in rural or town surroundings and those in urban or city surroundings(47). This has been interpreted(24) as showing a closeness to traditional middle-class values regarding work and achievement in the small-town factories in the sample, and an alienation from such values in the urban setting. Another group of researchers claims that while the workers in their study held views about the characteristics of their work which were very similar to those found elsewhere (particularly disliking monotony, pace, lack of autonomy, and lack of opportunity to use skill), the fact that they actually remained in these jobs showed that they brought an economic, instrumental orientation to the work and that its intrinsic characteristics were not very important to them(17).

Clearly the part played in all this by adaptation on the one

4

hand and by perception – which may be a form of adaptation – on the other has not yet been adequately charted. For instance, it is generally agreed that human beings need variety, but variety is very much a matter of perception. There is the frequently told story of the research worker who was watching a young girl putting small circles of cork into the tops of toothpaste tubes. 'Don't you get bored doing that all day?' she asked. And the girl looked up in complete surprise: 'Oh no! They come up different every time.' The values of the observer must to some extent influence whether he takes this to mean that her capacities are being utilised, or that she has adapted to a situation which would otherwise be intolerable; choices based on values cannot be avoided.

Clearly, too, differences in research findings are to some extent a function of differences in research methods. Sometimes the complexity and dynamics of a situation are better illustrated by a single case than by a number of surveys. A maintenance mechanic in a chemical process firm was being interviewed. It was an unstructured interview, during which no specific questions were asked, and for about two hours he talked freely about his job. At first he took a fairly instrumental line: 'All I'm interested in is the money. This firm pays well, and that's the only reason I stop here. What a working man wants from his job is the pay packet, and don't let anybody kid you about other fancy notions.'

Half an hour later he was talking about the firm, and discussed various things which he thought were wrong with it. The interviewer said nothing, but the mechanic seemed to think that he was being inconsistent, because he stopped himself. Then he said, 'Well, you see, when you get a bit older, and the kids are off your hands, and you've paid for the house, and your wife's got a washing machine – you don't need money so much any more and you find you start noticing the firm. And by God it can annoy you!'

Half an hour after that he said, 'You know – what I really like is when the machine goes wrong and *I'm* the one who knows how to put it right.'

It would be foolish to argue about which of these was his 'real' attitude: they were all real. Like the skins of an onion, most of these attitudes exist in most people, and the question is which of them gets tapped. It explains too why such conflicting evidence is thrown up by a good deal of research: the view one would take of this man's attitude would depend on when the interview was closed.

The present state of knowledge about work satisfaction therefore suggests two observations. In the first place, in a general sense, knowledge about the subject is incomplete, especially if the model of knowledge being used is that of engineering science. Human motivation will continue to provide material for doctoral theses for a long time. In themselves, attempts to draw up simple mechanical guidelines on how to deal with it deny the dynamic nature of the subject. In the absence of 'definitive' and 'complete' knowledge, therefore, ideas about psychological health are to some extent value-laden and will remain so, and choices have to be made. However, a good deal of understanding and experience exists about the consequences of such choices.

Secondly, in any specific situation one must take steps to explore the history, tradition, needs, and values of the people in the situation. The theoretician is left with a number of unknowns about human needs; the practitioner in a particular situation, however, has the means of finding out.

Consequences for culture

The current intense interest in job design has focussed very much on the effect of present forms of work organisation on the need satisfactions of individuals. It must be pointed out, however, that important effects can be seen at other behavioural levels. The way in which work is organised influences how people see and experience their surroundings; and the ways in which they experience and respond to things add up to strong and well-rooted cultures. These in turn then have consequences for society.

In a study of batch production of light engineering products(30), a big gulf was found to exist between the shopfloor operators and other people in the firm. This gulf was induced by the organisation of the work: differences in working experience led to differences in perception, attitudes, and behaviour. The firm, typical of the light engineering industry, manufactured a variety of products in batches of varying sizes. The work was rationalised and subdivided so that in the machine shops, on which the study was focussed, there were groups of milling machines, drilling machines, capstan lathes, etc., each performing one operation on a wide

6

variety of components. This form of work organisation was long established and the operators did not question or resent it. If there had ever been any opposition it had been resolved long ago, and they probably did not think that there could be any alternative way of organising work. They were fairly comfortable and fairly contented.

On the other hand there were strong indications that the way in which the work was organised had influenced them considerably. It influenced first of all their *perception*, especially their perception of 'the job'. 'The job' meant the immediate job cycle. When they talked about 'good' jobs as distinct from 'bad' jobs they meant jobs which had a loose price, jobs on which tools did not break easily or need sharpening too often, jobs on which production runs were long so that one could get into the swing of the job and make bonus, jobs which had been well inspected after the previous operation. One operator said, 'When I say it's a good job, I mean they're clean, they've been well inspected, there aren't a lot of burrs to catch your hands'. It showed a very restricted perception of 'the job'.

The operators did not resent changes which were going on in the firm, because these changes did not impinge on them and they were often not even aware of them. The firm might be introducing new products or devising new processes, but for the machine operator this could simply mean that he was drilling a hole of different dimensions in a different grade of metal with no indication of why. Therefore 'the job' had not changed.

This narrow definition of the job was reinforced by the piece-work system. If a man was paid every time he made a half-inch cut, the implication was that this was what the firm considered his job to be – not making a good product or being in any way concerned with the wider objectives of the firm.

The form of work organisation therefore also influenced *attitudes*. The operators on the whole regarded the firm as a good employer, but they were not very interested in it and did not feel personally involved in its affairs. The most frequent comment about the firm, and the main reason for liking it, was that it gave one a feeling of independence and freedom from close supervision; people were not breathing down one's neck all the time. A typical comment about the factory superintendent was: 'He doesn't get in my way and I don't get in his. That's how it should be.'

The market conditions within which the firm was operating and its economic and technical policies only affected the operators if they interfered – as they sometimes did – with the smooth running of the piecework system. It is a necessary condition of piecework that there must be enough work available, that tools must be in good supply and well maintained, and that the planning of production must be smooth and efficient. Otherwise piecework is felt to be unfair. Thus it became important, and there was considerable pressure, for management to keep the operators sheltered from the problems of the firm. These were in fact considerable, since the firm was engaged in small-batch production in a difficult market and had acute problems of how to deal with urgent orders, control production, decide optimum batch sizes, keep down stocks and decide stock levels, and adapt to market fluctuations.

The piecework system also postulated certain personality characteristics on the part of operators, and many in fact made the appropriate response. It was possible to describe and identify the 'ideal pieceworker', the man who fitted into the system most successfully and with least stress to himself:

A He had good physical health since the pace of work was high, and obviously the faster he worked the more he stood to gain.
B He was strongly motivated in the direction of money but not too much so. If his need for money was too urgent he might produce and record too much work and draw management's attention to loose prices.
C He was independent, the kind of person who did not want a close relationship with his superiors or a close involvement with his firm.
D He was confident vis-à-vis his superiors, having the courage to challenge prices and to hold his own in the battle with time study.
E He was not too troubled about the quality of the product or the care of tools. He was paid, after all, for output. If tools broke or faulty pieces got through to inspection, the payment system told him that this was not his concern.

Of course, not everyone had all these characteristics. There were a number of deviants: people who were old or in poor health and found the pace too hard; people who were nervous during a time study or did not dare to challenge prices; people who did not intend to stay in the firm and therefore did not care what prices they achieved; people with too great an interest in quality or tools;

8

people with an urgent need for a lot of money. Any of these could distort the pattern of prices or upset the manipulations of the booking system. But one could identify the ideal pieceworker, the person who was best adapted to this environment, and certainly many of the operators seemed to have made this kind of adaptation and justified management's assumption that all operators are like this.

Now one way of describing a culture is to describe the kind of individual who fits into it most successfully, and this brings us back to the main finding of this set of researches(10). In the short term the re-organisation of work and of payment systems could cause problems of adaptation and adjustment. In the long term they had the effect of creating a particular culture. For the operators in this firm the environment was consistent, requiring certain personality characteristics and tending to influence their perceptions and attitudes in certain directions. Life for them was fairly comfortable; they were preoccupied with the immediate job cycle and their bonus earnings, and they were not involved with or interested in the affairs of the firm. For everyone else, whose work was not yet highly rationalised, the demands of the environment were much more varied and conflicting; their perception was wider, and their attitudes were less homogeneous. Although their lives were much more rushed, harassed, and uncomfortable, they were interested in and concerned about the affairs of the firm and were considerably involved. (This included hourly paid checkers and bonus clerks, who were people selected on the same basis as operators but unable for some reason to stand the physical strain of operating machines – so their response is not likely to have been a function of intelligence or educational level.) The situation, therefore, also had the secondary effect of dividing the firm very clearly into two, the operators and the rest.

This may be the same phenomenon which Brown has described as 'the gap at the bottom of the executive system'(5). He attributes it, in the case of the Glacier Metal Company, to inadequate definition of one of the work roles in the system. But there would also seem to be logical reasons for it in the way work was organised and in the resulting conflicts of interest.

Organisational contexts;

If the organisation of work is interpreted in a rather wider frame of reference, then account needs to be taken of the relationships

9

between the task an organisation sets itself, the means it selects to carry out that task, and the human and social situations that result. A number of studies in the last fifteen years have suggested that there are some patterns and regularities in such relationships, that circumstances can be described in which some kinds of organisation are more effective than others, and that degrees of freedom to choose can be made explicit. Research has shown links between the forms and problems to be found in an organisation, sometimes even the characteristics of its industrial relations, and such structural factors as the kind of market in which a firm operates(6, 32, 34*), the technology it uses(15), the control systems it installs(52), and its size(38).

Again, the knowledge produced by such studies is not 'definitive' or 'conclusive'. There is need for a great deal more research based on detailed observation of what happens in real, not hypothetical, organisations. What this field of study has produced already, however, is guidelines for diagnosis. When a situation is examined with these relationships in mind and from the point of view of the interaction between structure and behaviour, there frequently emerges a new understanding of the situation which can serve as a basis for future action. Stresses and incompatibilities may become apparent which permit restructuring the situation or, if restructuring is not possible or acceptable, which at least make it clear why certain problems continue to recur.

Methods of organisational diagnosis need to go far beyond the conventional sociological tools of questionnaire and interview. Observation methods, tracer methods (tracing of product or other key unit through everything that happens to it in the organisation and analysing the work roles of all the people involved), activity sampling, analysis of documents, and depth analysis of roles all have a place in the equipment of applied social science. The main problems which are uncovered in this way may not in the first instance – or even at all – be those connected with tasks at the lowest level of the enterprise. But the systemic relationship between situations at different levels will become explicit, and strategies for change and development can be selected on a basis of knowledge.

* Lupton's research is mainly concerned with shopfloor response to incentives, but he shows incidentally that this response appears to differ in different market situations.

If I have so far approached the question of re-designing the work at the lowest level of the enterprise with some caution, and in the context of other kinds of organisational diagnosis, it is because the case is too important to risk damaging it by over-simplifying or over-stating it. Many tasks, particularly in industrial organisations and particularly at subordinate levels in these organisations, are unsatisfactory from the point of view of the personal needs, development, and even health of those who have to carry them out. This problem is at last attracting attention and there is much concern with reform. However, if reform is not carried out with an understanding of organisational contexts, the new structures will not work or will not last. Secondly, if the enthusiasm of reformers leads them to over-emphasise one factor in the situation (such as participation) at the expense of others (such as money, or security, or the needs of others than shopfloor operators) the next generation of reformers or researchers will pull down the whole edifice including the valuable parts of it. It is throwing out the baby with the bathwater, and in the field of applied social science there is already some experience of it. The excitement of a new discovery, particularly discovery of a way of righting something experienced as wrong, carries within it the seeds of its own destruction if it leads to exaggeration. F. W. Taylor himself, after all, the arch-priest and nowadays perhaps the arch-villain of 'scientific management', was only over-reacting to obvious inefficiencies which he witnessed – workers deciding how to produce a part guided only by their own skill and past experience, and holding their knowledge as trade secrets, with no concern for any wider systemic needs.

Enthusiasm which is not rooted in reality or, more usually, which is based on a partial view of reality, takes on the characteristics of an ideology, and there are many ideologies current in industry today: for management by objectives or M.B.O., for management information systems or M.I.S., etc. There must not be another fad called participative job design, or P.J.D. The nature of work is too important.

It is therefore valuable to look at some conclusions which were arrived at in a very non-ideological atmosphere. In 1970 the NATO Committee on the Challenges of Modern Society asked the United Kingdom to sponsor a study on problems of work motivation and satisfaction. Sponsorship was undertaken by the

U.K. Department of Employment, under the general guidance of the chief psychologist in the Research and Planning Division. The study was carried out by Dr N. A. B. Wilson, an industrial psychologist with long experience in industrial and military contexts. Here are his conclusions, quoted almost in full:

First, a prima facie case at the least has been made for regarding some features of a variety of modern work systems as stressful. These are chiefly: forced, uniform pacing, especially if the pace is high; repetitiveness and very short time cycles, leading to monotony, triviality and meaninglessness in work; large impersonal structures of organisation, working arrangements and relations; objectives which seem distant and unreal to the worker (even if in fact vital to him). Major gains in occupational life have accrued from exploitation of just these features, but a stage of diminishing returns is reached with industrial maturity.

Secondly, there exists a wide consensus among people closely concerned with systematic study of working life (physiologists, social scientists, occupational medical men, and at least some industrial relations experts) that the stresses just mentioned (pace, monotony, size, anonymity, etc.) are real in their effects. They make work less attractive to enter and less satisfying to do. They lead to problems of undermanning, absence, labour turnover, defects and suchlike outcomes of attitudes which, being not fully engaged, easily become less than responsible. Besides the consensus, there is a good deal of experimental evidence to justify such conclusions. The connection with poor hourly productivity or with industrial conflict or even with loss of output due to accidents has not been empirically demonstrated; although it is easy to suppose that work which conveys chiefly feelings of deprivation can lead to attitudes of apathy or aggression and a will to extract the maximum extrinsic compensation. (It is probably not sufficiently realised how much workers as a group feel that the products of industry are 'theirs' personally and that the contributions of employers, organisers and staff people generally are subsidiary, or even marginal.)

Thirdly, as people become better off and better educated, or at the least see their fellows becoming so, and levels of expectation of all kinds are raised, it becomes increasingly necessary to take account of demands for satisfaction, scope, opportunities for exercising skills, etc. in working life. Advertisements in the newspapers and public places have been showing the trend for some time now, and employers and other designers of work are going to have to meet the substance of such claims, otherwise they may find their other costs prohibitive. What is needed is the use of as much effort and ingenuity in devising schemes for stimulation, self-organising activity and feeling of day-to-day achievement in work as has hitherto been devoted to schemes for coercion, control and detailing of tasks. Improvements must come mainly through 'work structuring' in its wider sense.

Fourthly, there have been quite convincing demonstrations (in perhaps forty or fifty published accounts) that modern work systems can be revised to meet the needs of a competitive economy while at the same time affording a range of jobs which are at the least comparatively satisfying and progressive for most of the people available to do them. These do not appear to be utopian or ephemeral though none has yet attained more than modest size, usually within the perimeter of an established concern. The urge to plan and develop them has typically come from a mixture of economic, philanthropic and (social) scientific motives, in varying proportions. For the present at least, their success depends upon the expertise and commitment of key personnel and a positive willingness, or at least beneficent neutrality, from others concerned. When greatly extended this sort of thing should lead to the full utilisation of human resources for the attainment of shared benefits.

In the fifth place, social science research and applications have an essential part, for the forseeable future, in such developments as they are undertaken. It need hardly be added that the role of social science must be a diminishing one in each individual case as it progresses towards self-sustaining operation . . . (50)

2. Assumptions, values, and responses in work organisation

Rationalised production

For more than 150 years, the choices made in the design and organisation of work have tended to be in the direction of rationalisation, specialisation and the sub-division of tasks, and the minimising and standardising of skills. With every new discovery of science the intellectual excitement surrounding the discovery very quickly gives way to the equally exciting search for ways of making use of it, either by incorporating it into new products or into new techniques or processes. Thus, first in manufacture and later in administration, the knowledge and methods of the natural sciences have been put to the task of discovering methods of working and organising which would give economical and predictable results.

In this search, the criteria have been the twin ones of economic benefit on the one hand and predictability and control on the other. In the process, as many critics have pointed out, some other criteria came to be neglected. But before moving on to this topic an important point needs to be made about the origin of design criteria. Critics have often blamed greed and an excessive emphasis on commercial gain for the harmful effects of scientific management. Davis(11) made a study of the criteria and practices currently used by those involved in job design in the United States, obtaining seven interviews and twenty-four questionnaire responses from manufacturing firms. Although the sample was small and the industries diverse, the responses obtained were highly consistent and are probably even more significant when one considers that the organisations responding to these enquiries were likely to be those having an explicit interest in work organisation or job design. Among the summary of his findings are the following on design criteria:

The content of individual tasks is specified

A   so as to achieve specialisation of skills,
B   so as to minimise skill requirements,
C   so as to minimise learning time or operator training time,
D   so as to equalise and permit the assignment of a full workload,
E   in a manner which provides operator satisfaction (no specific criteria for job satisfaction were found in use), and
F   as dictated by considerations of layout of equipment or facilities and, where they exist, of the union restrictions on work assignment.

Individual tasks are combined into specific jobs so that

A   specialisation of work is achieved whenever possible by limiting the number of tasks in a job and limiting the variations in tasks or jobs,
B   the content of the job is as repetitive as possible, and
C   training time is minimised.

Davis points out that these criteria are governed by consideration for the immediate cost of performing the required operation, while the total long-term economic costs of a job design are not taken into account. Ideas about human asset accounting are in their infancy.

It must be remembered, however, that other assumptions and anxieties of engineering designers, besides those concerned with costs, play a part in the process as well. Engineers often attribute to economy innovations which are really made for reasons of control, and control systems themselves are often inadequately costed. It is deeply rooted in science and engineering training that knowledge means measurement and control, and the human sciences are thought to be immature or inadequate in so far as they do not produce the kind of knowledge which makes human material as predictable or controllable as chemical material.

Because of this tradition and this training base, the less easily measurable aspects of human behaviour create anxiety for engineers, who have therefore tended to make use in their design thinking of only those human characteristics to which engineering-type measures could be applied – selection tests for aptitudes, fatigue allowances incorporated into incentive schemes for reward, more recently statistical projections for manpower planning, etc. There is a tendency for the precision and validity of such measures to be over-estimated, while the precision and validity of, for instance, experience are under-estimated.

Engineering designers know, of course, that human beings have other characteristics as well, but they have great difficulty in integrating this knowledge with their other knowledge, to make it part of their operating reality. Quite non-threatening aspects of human dynamics – for instance, the fact that people set themselves sub-targets in order to experience achievement and measure progress (with its implications for batch size) or that they do not work at a constant pace throughout the day but vary their working pace (with its implications for buffer stocks)(9) – have not found their way into design strategies. Where they are allowed for, it is generally by accident. An intuitive awareness that important aspects of human behaviour have not been allowed for in production design probably makes the designer experience the people in the system as a puzzling if not threatening factor. In recent years the growing power of organised labour, too, has no doubt added to this anxiety. As a result, an engineering designer is likely to feel most pleased that he has found a design solution when he has designed a human operator out of the system altogether, frequently in situations in which this answer is not the most economical one or the one which makes the system work best. Controls are often left permanently on 'manual' by people with operating experience of what a system really needs.

Responses to rationalised production

A number of responses to this situation can be identified.

Criticism

At an intuitive and descriptive level, rationalised production methods have been criticised for a very long time. Marx produced some detailed critical descriptions of the work carried out by people in a number of different technologies and the effects on personal and social life. The conclusions he drew, however, were not about the design of jobs but about ownership and about macro-economic structures.

W. F. Taylor's book on 'scientific management'(43) was published in 1911. As early as 1915 there appeared a detailed critique based on an investigation of scientific management in its relation to labour, made for the United States Commission on Industrial Relations by R. F. Hoxie(23). It involved the study of scientific management shops, designated in the main by Taylor, Gantt, and Emerson. Hoxie was assisted by an expert representing employing management and an expert representing labour. After reading the literature and holding discussions with the leaders of opinion on both sides he prepared two documents, one on the labour claims of scientific management and one on the trade union objections to it. On the basis of this an extensive questionnaire covering about a hundred pages was prepared and sent to the scientific management firms for their reply. These firms were visited and on the basis of the discussions and answers to the questionnaire the book was written.

The date of publication makes this a fascinating work, and extracts from it are included as Appendix 1. The fact that it appears to have had almost no impact at the time, the nature of its conclusions, and the fact that these conclusions are very similar to those drawn by social and other scientists today, have important implications. There is criticism of unsubstantiated claims to 'science', of poorly trained practitioners jumping on to the band-wagon set in motion by more responsible workers in the field, of over-simplifying and lumping together methods which in fact vary considerably – criticisms which are relevant to other 'movements' as well as to that of scientific management. All this is in addition to discussion of the effects of these techniques which are more what one would expect: that the economic benefits are very great, that the social effects are not the beneficial ones claimed but are in fact frequently harmful, and that ways must be sought to retain the first while reversing the harm done by the second.

Accommodation

There are many ways in which workers have dealt with the production situations in which they find themselves. These may include accepting and sharing the value systems which underlie the production organisation, withdrawing attention from it and becoming apathetic, saving their energies for the non-work aspects of life, etc. The kind of accommodation to which I want to draw attention here is the one which finds areas of freedom and control within the work situation itself. There are very many cases where, precisely because the methods of 'scientific' management are not as scientific as all that, loopholes exist which have enabled workers to regain a considerable measure of control over their own work situation. Individual piecework is a good example: in many industries it is popular, not only because of the possibility of high earnings, but also because it makes people to some extent responsible for their own earnings, frees them from close personal supervision, and gives them a feeling of independence. In addition, the process of deciding the time for a job is itself susceptible to manipulation, and the battle of wits with time study has the function of adding stimulus to an otherwise dull work situation. There may also be considerable opportunities to optimise one's personal resources of time and energy in the way that output is recorded. The pieceworker who works very hard on Thursdays, saves the pieces overnight, and feeds them in on Fridays so as not to be too tired for the weekend is, after all, being entirely rational.

This has obvious implications for re-design activities. Attempts to introduce new freedoms may interfere with areas of freedom which already exist. Even with the introduction of flexi-time, situations have arisen where the new flexibility has destroyed flexibility which the people in the situation had informally arranged for themselves. This is yet another reason for reiterating the need for detailed and realistic diagnosis of existing situations where re-design activities are envisaged. It also emphasises the difference, theoretically and methodologically, between re-design and new design which will be discussed in more detail later. Finally it points to the need for experience, flexibility, and sensitivity on the part of practitioners who get involved in re-design activities. There seems little value in replacing the solutions of rigid and doctrinaire production engineering with those of rigid and doctrinaire social science.

There seems to be one important exception in this process of accommodation. While in practice many situations fall short of scientific management's aims of detailed and complete control over the operator, the paced assembly line in mass-production has taken these aims to their logical conclusion and seems to have generally defeated informal manipulation. It has come to symbolise the subjection of man to mechanical control. For this reason the current experiments of Volvo and Saab Scania have a symbolic and political significance which is far greater than that of any other current experiment. As one Swede triumphantly put it, 'If these experiments work, after 1975 it will simply not be possible to build any more assembly lines!'

Continuing enthusiasm

In this discussion it must be remembered that the main trend in the design of work organisation continues to be in the direction of specialisation and external control. Although there are a growing number of experiments in other directions, nowhere has 'critical mass', or anything like it, been achieved for alternatives. What is growing steadily is an awareness that current work design has disadvantages from some points of view. Those who have experience of existing technology, and who are in everyday contact with operators and with production problems, are frequently very willing to acknowledge this and very ready to consider ways of modifying existing systems. Their main problems stem from the fact that large sums are already invested in the existing systems.

It is truly tragic, then, to see the same mistakes being made in the design of new technology. The overriding enthusiasm engendered in young designers by new technical possibilities, such as automatic process control or data processing, has led in some instances to the same attitudes of omnipotence as inspired the early industrial engineers. Very large projects are designed by computer consultants in swift succession, and the career development pattern for systems analysts has been such that they often do not stay in a position long enough to learn about the operational problems that ensue.

In process control, there are subtle but important differences according to whether tasks are designed so that operators monitor the process – i.e. respond automatically to signals which leave only one course of action open – or control it – i.e. respond to symptoms and make decisions about action. The differences, and the skills which are in reality still required, are not always recognised. It is essential that operators understand the process, recognise faults or impending faults, and know what to do about them. A study of training needs for automation(28) analysed a number of cases of breakdown and revealed that the judgement and skill required from operators had not been understood when the process was set up. Sounder on-the-spot decisions by operators, based on a more skilful analysis of the factors involved, could have saved expensive breakdowns.

Research on computer-based information systems points out that every system design contains an implied model of the user, and that this model may be inadequate and is likely to be influenced by professional ideologies(3). Three kinds of model which can be discerned from existing systems are (a) that the user is wholly rational and knows what he needs (which is like asking someone if he wants an apple when he has never seen or tasted one), (b) that the user is wholly irrational and should be designed out of the system, and (c) that it must be optimal to routinise existing systems (which is like saying that since a horse is a means of transport and a lorry is a means of transport, every horse should be replaced by a lorry and all side effects will be beneficial).

So-called 'decision rules' imply that the user is a mechanism, and that all that is needed is to design a system which outputs details of the action the user is to take. At the other extreme, the assumption is that the user is the best judge of the information he needs. Neither of these assumptions matches reality. Much more complex assumptions and models of reality have to be postulated, and this means that development needs to be in terms of much more highly interactive systems: systems must interact with their own past, i.e. development must be evolutionary and build on what happened before; and systems must interact with the user. This is the only fruitful way of making the best use of the two resources, (a) of a complex model of man, and (b) of the systems designer who appreciates what formal information systems are capable of doing. Without such interaction, on a continuing basis, the goals and values implied by the systems which are produced are not necessarily those intended by the users.

Rejection of technology

In the last fifty years there have developed two manifestations of a flight from technology. The first took the form of the 'human relations movement'. It has its roots in the work of Elton Mayo and the Hawthorne experiments(40), which drew attention to social relations as an important factor in the work situation. As a result there have been considerable attempts, particularly in the United States, to modify the behavioural styles of supervisors and managers and the quality of personal relationships at work, usually through sensitivity training or through the intervention of a so-called 'change agent' in working situations.

This kind of training and intervention, however, tends to focus exclusively on relationships, treating the social system as self-contained, and to pay little attention to tasks, either the task of an organisation as a whole or those of individuals. At best it is hoped that individuals who in this way become sensitised to relationships at the work place, will themselves begin to direct a new kind of attention to their tasks. Experience frequently shows, however, that such individuals become fascinated by their new human relations experiences and want to continue developing them, sometimes drawing even further away from considerations of task and technology. It can happen, therefore, that organisations simultaneously pursue human relations programmes which emphasise open, participative, and democratic styles of behaviour, and industrial engineering or other management service programmes aimed at centralising and tightening control and closing up loopholes. The difficulty of bridging this gulf between the wish and the reality is not made easier by the sophistication of many managers nowadays who, in the Anglo-Saxon countries at any rate, are familiar with the human relations literature and talk with ease of 'Theory Y'(35) and 'System 4'(33) and '9–9 Management'(4).

The second manifestation of the rejection of technology is more recent, more internally consistent, and more relevant to the European situation: it is the fact that many young people, whose education has been longer in duration and less authoritarian in style than that of their parents and who do not have memories of economic hardship, simply do not want to work in industry. Their years at school have not prepared them for work which is subordinate, monotonous, and lacking in self-direction and the use of skill. It is this which lends urgency to the need to reconsider the organisation of industrial work and it is indeed this which underlies many of the experiments which are already going on, particularly the widespread programme of experimentation which is going on in Sweden.

Research

Research on the relations between the technical and human aspects of production systems goes back to the early 1920s(48, 54, 18). Studies carried out by members of the Tavistock Institute of Human Relations from the late 1940s onwards were in this tradition but had a number of additional distinguishing features:

A they led to new and important kinds of conceptualisation;
B they incorporated analyses of social organisation which were based on research and experimentation in group functioning;
C they were programmatic – that is a body of inter-related concepts, theories, and methods was (and is being) developed and tested in the course of a number of inter-related studies. This must not be seen in a romantic light, as there were in fact many setbacks, problems of sanction and finance, etc. But it is an important point to remember when one is considering institutional bases for research;
D the social scientists were not merely observers but were actively involved in experimental change. There were two kinds of action role, that of the action-researcher and that of the consultant. The methodological examination of these roles formed part of the research.

Most of the basic concepts in the field of socio-technical systems study* can be traced back to a paper by Trist and Bamforth(45) on the social and psychological consequences of the long-wall method of coal-getting.

In the coal-face studied, the cycle of coal-getting involved three operations:

A preparation, concerned with making the coal more accessible and workable;
B getting, in which the coal was loaded and transported away from the face;
C advancing, in which roof supports, gateway haulage roads, and conveyor equipment were advanced.

Mechanisation had been introduced with the expectation of achieving a higher level of productivity. As a result the traditional small, self-regulating, and independent teams, which had together carried out the total cycle, were broken up. The new system required for its operation forty to fifty men, each working on a single task. The work organisation which resulted was one in which the different teams were now working independently in shifts, each on different piece rates, but by the nature of the task

* The rest of this chapter, and the first three parts of chapter 3, draw heavily on the writings of members of the Tavistock Institute of Human Relations, London, and the Work Research Institute, Oslo. The source documents for the remainder of this chapter are (20) and (46).

dependent on one another to get their work done. Each of these teams of workers, optimising conditions for itself, created and passed on poor conditions to the work groups responsible for subsequent tasks. Instead of enabling them to co-operate with one another, the new system created irresolvable conditions for inter-personal and inter-group conflict, resulting in competitive individualism, mutual scapegoating, and a high level of absenteeism, all of which contributed to a low level of productivity. At the same time all the controlling and co-ordinating activities now had to come from outside and above the teams, since no one at the workface knew the whole story.

The concept which began to emerge at this stage of the research was that if one optimises the technical system at the expense of the social system, the results achieved will be sub-optimal. (The same would be true if one attempted to optimise the social system at the expense of the technological system. Where conflicts are built into a work organisation there is little that can be achieved by a human relations approach to conflict resolution.)

The second series of coal mining studies was concerned with carrying out more systematic and, where possible, quantitative studies. In the course of field work in the Durham area a number of composite autonomous work groups were discovered, which had been organised by the men themselves with the co-operation of the pit manager. Comparative studies with conventional work organisations consistently showed the superiority of composite autonomous work organisations, in terms of both productivity and social–psychological criteria. The most interesting of these were long-wall faces where the total group of more than forty men working on a three-shift cycle had organised themselves as an autonomous group. Cohesion was in this case maintained by a work rotation scheme which had evolved both within and between shifts. It became clear at this stage that a single technological system can still allow for a choice, at least within a range of feasible social systems.

The possibilities of socio-technical analysis, and the possibility of exercising organisational choice, marked an important turning point in the development of work organisation.

3. New thinking in work organisation

Exercising organisational choice – A case study

The first explicit attempt to design and implement a socio-technical system was made by Rice in 1953 at the Calico Mills at Ahmedabad in India(39). The following is his own summary of the experimental changes carried out in an automatic loom shed, and part of his summary of subsequent experiments in a non-automatic loom shed.

The automatic loom shed

The weaving process of an automatic loom shed had been broken down into component tasks and the number of workers allocated to each separate component had been determined by work studies.

The resultant pattern was that of an aggregate of individuals with confused task and role relationships and with no discernible internal group structure.

Higher management had reinforced the management of the shed. This, together with the quality of the relationships among the supervisors, and between them and the workers, had prevented any overt difficulties arising from the lack of group structure. Nevertheless efficiency was lower and damage higher than target figures. Productivity was in fact no better than with non-automatic looms.

In spite of the persistence of 'weaver' as a title for an occupational role, the weaver was now the loom and all workers including the 'weavers' serviced machines.

The tasks performed could be differentiated into two main groups: those concerned with weaving, and those concerned with loading (gating) and loom maintenance. There were in addition only minor ancillary services.

An analysis of changes in the number of workers according to sort* woven showed that stable numbers could be maintained for each of three main categories – coarse, medium and fine. Provided some tasks could be made inter-changeable, no changes in work group numbers would be required for changes within a main sort. The theoretical numbers required for blocks of 64 looms into which the loom shed was divided by physical boundaries could be calculated.

Three natural grades within a work group for 64 looms were found, instead of the nine grades existing. They were designated by letters only; rates slightly in excess of existing rates were fixed, and it was decided to pay piece rates to the whole group.

Shed supervisors and workers spontaneously took possession of the reorganisation, the workers themselves immediately organising four experimental groups. Higher management took no part in the discussions with supervisors and workers, and permitted the experimental groups so chosen to start work.

The immediate results of the experiment were:

A the creation of internally structured and internally led small work groups;
B a reduction in the number of those reporting directly to the supervisor and a consequent strengthening of the executive command;
C the beginning of the withdrawal of higher management from the managing system of the shed;
D the abandonnment of old titles but without the emergence of new; letter grades only being used;
E after an immediate increase in efficiency in the experimental groups at the cost of increased damage and inadequate maintenance, a settling down at a new level of performance at which efficiency was higher and damage lower than before reorganisation.

When the form of organisation was extended to the rest of the shed and a third shift started, the efficiency was maintained for several months but in October and November 1953 it dropped steeply through a period of five weeks. At the same time the figures for damage rose steadily.

Investigation showed that:

* Sort = type of cloth woven, defined by thickness of yarn, and by the number of threads to the inch in both warp and weft.

A each group had had to contend with variations in the sort woven;

B there had been insufficient spare workers to provide extra help for increased loom stoppage rates and loss of time;

C extension and expansion at the same time had given insufficient opportunity for adequate training either of new or of existing workers in the new methods of organisation;

D the intended concentration of training in two groups had not been possible and training had been diffused throughout all groups;

E the basis on which the original experimental groups had been formed had not allowed sufficient time for group leaders to perform the task of leading;

F as a result of the difficulties caused by these factors, group members had regressed to earlier working habits more appropriate to individual than to group working.

Action was taken:

A to establish basic rates of pay;

B to re-shuffle the groups into production, transition, and training groups;

C to close down enough groups to allow adequate time for training, and to provide spare workers for increased stoppage rates;

D to erect two looms apart from a shed to train new and existing workers in the basic skills of loom running and maintenance;

E to implement the policy of keeping a group on the same sort for as long as possible, confining experimental sorts to whole groups rather than spreading them over all groups;

F to locate in the shed managing system appropriate and necessary control functions.

The beginning of the investigation and the establishment of minimum rates of pay coincided with a halt in the drop in efficiency and in the rise of damage. Thereafter the efficiency of production and transition groups rose and quality showed continuous improvement . . .

It was concluded that the first spontaneous acceptance of the new system and the subsequent determination to make it work were due primarily to the workers' intuitive acceptance of it as one which would provide them with the security and protection of small group membership, which they had left by leaving their villages and their families to enter industry. At the same time the new system allowed them to perform their primary task effectively, and that provided them with an important source of satisfaction.

Non-automatic weaving

In a subsequent experiment (1953–4) group methods of working were extended to non-automatic weaving. Again, the emphasis lay on modifying the social organisation by creating interdependent and internally structured working groups, with occasional minor modifications to the technology to make this possible. Here are some – even more condensed – extracts:

Studies of the existing production system showed that:

A Weavers who each ran two looms were in their formal role relationships independent isolates. Informally they made supportive and mutually helpful relationships with each other, taking over each other's looms so that they could spend long periods outside the sheds.
B Weavers, who were responsible for the quality and quantity of cloth woven, were subject to the authorities of three departments: their own, the Preparatory Department and the Sales Department. They had frequently to visit other parts of the mill to obtain weft yarn and to deliver woven cloth.
C In spite of multiple authorities and a wide range of movement, weavers performed an integrated 'whole' task, the conversion of yarn to cloth.
D Two supervisors of equal status were in charge of each shift of each loom shed. There was confusion about their responsibilities and authority. In addition neither of them had any authority over some parts of the weaving process...

An experimental shed was set up staffed by applicants from existing loom sheds. In the experimental shed:

A all looms were fitted with warp-stop motions;
B the tasks of weaving were differentiated as to task area, time period, skill, and condition;
C the tasks of loom-running were further differentiated into
(1) front work – shuttling and warp mending from the front of

the loom, and (2) back work – fault prevention and warp
mending from the back;

D small internally structured work groups were constituted to
perform all the tasks of weaving and maintenance on groups of
40 looms, all of which wove the same kind of cloth
continuously;

E the members of the work groups performed interdependent
tasks and formed interdependent relationships.

Minimum basic rates were fixed higher than had previously
been paid. Four natural grades within a work group were found:
group leader, front loom worker, back loom worker, and helper.
Bonus was paid both for quantity and quality; fining for bad
quality was stopped. The bonus was paid, at the workers' own
request, for group rather than for individual performance.

All tasks related to weaving, including inspection, were made
the responsibility of the senior supervisor in charge of the loom
shed. Standards of inspection were agreed after a joint inspection
of some hundreds of yards of cloth by the senior supervisor, shift
supervisors, inspectors, and group leaders. Self inspection and self
criticism were accepted by management as imposing higher
standards of inspection and better quality control than when
inspection was a function of the Sales Department.

The experimental period lasted ten months. The outcome
during the first weeks was confused by the quality of some
equipment, difficulties with humidification, and the inexperience
of both workers and supervisors with the new methods.
Improvements were made in the equipment; the loom stoppage
rates were partially controlled by variations in the speed of
looms. Both management and workers 'tested out' each other's
sincerity and willingness to co-operate. Gradually, permissive and
collaborative relationships based on mutual trust were built up.

The building of permissive and collaborative relationships
between management and workers and the stabilising of
intra-group relationships were assisted by the institution of
informal group meetings and of more formal conferences [at
which] the whole executive chain responsible for production was
present. At first separate conferences were held for the different
shifts but at the workers' request all shifts attended the same
conferences which were held partly in the first shift and partly in

the second. When a third shift was started the workers on this shift willingly came in, in their own time, to attend...

After a very slow start the efficiency of the shed climbed steadily...until during the ninth and final phase of the experimental period it was somewhat higher than equivalent efficiencies in other loom sheds. The quality of the cloth woven in the experimental shed, after being worse than that woven in other sheds for the first phase, steadily improved...and finally settled down at a better standard than was achieved in other sheds.

The immediate practical result of the experiment has been to demonstrate that the breakdown of the 'whole' task of weaving into component operations, each performed by a different worker, and the reintegration of the workers into an internally structured work group that performs the 'whole' task on a group of looms can be accomplished in one process provided that permissive and collaborative relationships can be built up between all those concerned.

The workers earned an average bonus of 28 per cent during the ninth phase of the experimental period; the mean earnings of the group were 55 per cent higher than the equivalent mean earnings in other sheds...The cost of the experimental shed was 13 per cent higher than the cost of an equivalent number of looms in other sheds. The output was 21 per cent higher and the number of damages 59 per cent less. These results were achieved on the most difficult sort regularly woven in the mills.

A new frame of reference – Industrial democracy

It will be clear that the dominant frame of reference in these experiments was that of social organisation. The main focus of intervention was at this level, not in order to optimise the social system independently of the technology, but in order to define tasks and work roles so that they met technical requirements while being more congruent with emerging knowledge about role relationships, interdependence, and leadership roles. At the same time Rice himself was acting as consultant to the top management of the concern, which was a family firm, about their own roles and relationships. This undoubtedly also influenced the support which was given to the experiments in the weaving sheds.

The next phase in the development and application of socio-technical theory came within a rather different frame of reference. In 1962 the Norwegian Confederation of Employers (NAF) and the Trade Union Congress of Norway (LO) set up a joint committee to consider questions of industrial democracy. The committee felt that these questions required social-scientific research, and a programme of research and experimentation was undertaken by the Institute for Industrial Social Research, Trondheim, which sought the collaboration of the Tavistock Institute. Later the research was transferred to the Work Research Institutes in Oslo when the former head of the Institute for Industrial Social Research, Professor Einar Thorsrud, became the head of this new Institute.

The general objective of the programme was to explore the question: 'Under what conditions can more rights and responsibilities be achieved for the individual in the work place?' A two-pronged research programme was developed:

Phase A – a study of existing Norwegian and other European experiences with mechanisms that allow formally for employee representation at top management level.

Phase B – a study of the roots of industrial democracy in the conditions for personal participation in the work place.

Phase A was completed, and the report published, in 1964 (English translation 1969)(15).

The joint committee and the research team were agreed that the second line of research, the study of personal participation, was of basic interest. They were convinced by existing evidence that the manner in which employees participate in the work life of their companies is critical for the use they make of formal mechanisms for representation and consultation and also for their attitudes of constructive interest, of satisfaction and dissatisfaction. They felt that 'the bulk of the scientific evidence suggests that the more the individual is enabled to exercise control over his task and to relate his efforts to those of his fellows the more likely is he to accept a positive commitment. This positive commitment shows in a number of ways not the least of which is the release of that personal initiative and creativity which constitutes the basis of a democratic climate.'*

* Op. cit. p. 100.

After considerable public discussion of the report on Phase A, and having regard to the industrial structure, the political and industrial relations history, and the educational system in Norway, it was then felt to be appropriate to proceed with Phase B, a programme of planned experimental changes.

The relationship between the researchers and the organisations in which they worked was differerent from that between Rice and the Calico Mills. Rice worked 'within a consultant–client relationship, in which my primary professional responsibility was to give such assistance as I could to the solution of problems causing concern to the client'.* The researchers in Norway were responsible to the joint committee of the NAF and LO, which financed the research, acted as consultative body for it, took part in the selection of research sites, and undertook to appraise the relevance of the research results for present Norwegian conditions and to help to make the results of the research work known and used. Thus their roles in the organisations themselves were those of action-researchers.

The basic concept was that of the enterprise as an open socio-technical system. This implies:

A The analysis of the component parts [of the enterprise] to reveal the nature of each, insofar as it contributes to the performance of the enterprise and creates or meets the requirements of other parts. The first components to be distinguished for purposes of analysis are:
  1 the technological;
  2 the 'work relationship structure' and its constituent occupational roles.
B The analysis of the inter-relation of these parts with particular reference to the problems of internal co-ordination and control thus created for the enterprise.
C The detection and analysis of the relevant external environment of the enterprise, and the manner in which the enterprise manages its relations to it.(13)

In early 1964 two companies, Christiania Spigerverk A/S, Oslo, and Hunsfos Fabrikker A/S, Vennesla, were selected for experimenting within the metal manufacturing industry and the pulp and paper industry. Later the project was extended to include

* Op. cit. p. 7.

experiments in the electrical panels department of the A/S Nobø Fabrikker at Hommelvik (1965) and in several production departments of A/S Norsk Hydro's chemical plant at Herøya (1967).

The report on Phase B is expected to be published shortly. Meanwhile, a number of accounts of different aspects of it are available, including an interim report on the whole project which Jan Irgens Karlsen prepared in 1972 (27).

Brief accounts cannot of course do justice to the complexity of the analyses which were carried out, both before and at various stages during the experiments. The following is a highly condensed account of two of them, given by Emery in 1967(14). It conveys some of the interest and intellectual challenge involved in reconsidering work to meet new standards and criteria:

In the wire drawing experiment, we did most of the job ourselves. Julius Marek together with Per Engelstad (chemist) and Knut Lange (metallurgist), who had done a year of social science at Oslo University, did a detailed examination of the technical system and the possibilities arising within it. Briefly what happens is this: thick wire is run at a very high speed through a set of reducing dies, finally emerging in a thin coil which is bundled away. The machinery required is designed in such a way that the supervision and handling is seen as a one-man job. Wire drawing seems to be done like this in all countries.

Engineers, although they have a choice in the design of the machinery, invariably seem to favour that system requiring this sort of organisation – i.e. one man in charge. But an examination of the workload involved shows the following pattern: most of the time the man is literally doing nothing. In fact, he is probably sitting down reading a comic or paper behind his bench and out of sight of everyone else. Then suddenly the wire breaks, and he is the only man available. There is some handling and inspection, and a little welding, but basically the pattern of activity fails to meet the criteria of optimal workload and variety.

There is no way of modifying the old pattern in the situation of one man/one machine. It was necessary to redesign the work so that a group of men took responsibility for a group of machines. In order to do this, it was necessary to make detailed calculations of the performance of each one of these machines, and of the men, to determine the appropriate work-load and its variance.

Having done this, and got agreement from management and

men for a three month experiment, we ran into a number of difficulties. We were unable to establish all the desired experimental conditions except for a period of about two weeks. This was largely due to the fact that the men just could not believe that they were not being sold down the river by their union leadership – more work for less money. In the end, when they saw the results, they realised just what they could do working as a group. As far as the technical side was concerned, there was practically no extra expenditure by the company on machinery or equipment, though we did manage, with difficulty, to get certain very cheap modifications introduced into the control system for stopping the machines.

We then ran into a rather peculiar problem. If the wire drawing men were given fair payment for the production they achieved as a result of group working, they would be among the highest paid men in the plant. So there would then be the problem of what to do about the status of the currently highest paid workers. Everyone couldn't be jacked up because the plant as a whole wasn't producing any more, and in fact, at the national level, this would have entailed a violation of the nationally agreed rates. (Norway, like Sweden, negotiates these at two-yearly intervals.)

The men in the wire mill recognised this difficulty and proposed that they be paid in time off; however, this too presented a problem because the Employers' Federation did not want to be confronted with a 40-hour week too rapidly.

From the beginning, both management and unions had been prepared to accept a significant gain on the social side, even if there had been no increase in productivity. Neither they nor we had fully realised the difficulties created by extra productivity. The problem has still not been resolved, though the company has set up an action group of its own people to get to work in other departments and move them in the same direction.

In reaction to this successful experiment and frustrating outcome, the union leadership decided that even if it took them 10 years or so, they would push their people to work along these lines, though this would entail training their men over from work study procedures and an overwhelming attachment to individual incentive rates.

Once the wire drawing experiment was under way, we were able to start on the pulp/paper mill, do an analysis of the overall situation and try to identify the key position for experimentation. This turned out to be the chemical pulp department. Here the problem was rather different from our past experience and for us most exciting. The technology was of a sort we had not experimented with before. The main task was information-handling requiring a high degree of technical skill. The physical effort involved in the jobs was negligible. A large range of informational flows had to be handled, not only within, but also between shifts, since the batches took, on average, about 16 hours to run. Responsibility for a batch had to be shared between shifts and could not simply be carried by a face-to-face group of operators.

The existing situation was not very reassuring. Although this was one of the largest mills in Norway at the time, the production was out of control for an extraordinary proportion of batches, that is, outside the technical quality control limits they themselves accepted as appropriate. This was not reflected in the quality of the final products but in the cost of achieving this end quality.

Building up a social system to carry this information presented us with a nice challenge, because we could think of only two other examples where this had been tackled. Some years ago an oil company in the States developed small size refineries for location near their markets. Thayer published a brief report on how these men were trained in groups. There had to be a sense of team leadership or the plants could not have been operated correctly, as they were so highly sensitive to loss of control and damage if information flows were not adequately handled. This lesson had been learned from the US Navy when nuclear submarines were introduced. The ordinary crew system was useless given the speed and way in which these craft could move under water, and information systems of a much higher order of capacity had to be developed. Thus the Navy, with rather more money to spend than most firms have at their disposal, built up their teams most assiduously on simulated models before they let the men anywhere near these tremendously expensive high-speed submarines where one false move could send them straight to the bottom.

These projects, we knew, had been relatively successful, so we pitched in and the experiment is now well under way. An interesting thing here was that our changes could be made only by introducing changes in the technical basis of the information system and the learning of the operators. Thus, unlike the wire drawing experiment, it would *not* be possible after three months' trial to stop the experiment, revert to the old-type working, and sit down and negotiate the results. The experimental changes would be continuous and not easily reversed, and hence had to be carefully tested and negotiated at each step.

Role of the foreman

During the course of our analysis of the pulp/paper situation, we examined the role of the foreman. At first glance he appeared to be fully occupied with work that seemed to be meaningful; however, when the activity was viewed from the other side (the technical side), we found that the key informational flow by-passed him. (This is clearly a Parkinsonian phenomenon. Put in four foremen, give them the men, and they will find four foremen's jobs for themselves.) But in this system, the men cannot be expected to take greater responsibility for the control they exercise, unless the possibility of further effective communication is established. A lot of our effort at this stage was spent in selecting appropriate points for instrumentation, deciding what kind of instrumentation was required and devising techniques for summarising information through the flow, information the men had not previously handled. Some information must be carried forward with each batch wherever it goes; the information also has to be carried over from one shift to another. This requires the development of summarising techniques so that the men can examine the effects of any actions they might take. With these developments it has become possible for the men to take ever increasing responsibility for the plant and thus bring production under control.

Our experience with this particular experiment suggested some general thoughts. When a position is reached where a technical system in its interaction with the social system is, generally speaking, out of control, then, as in a military situation, a very special type of leadership carrying entire responsibility is required. It is not possible to establish this military pattern in an industrial situation. Thus in the pulp/paper experiment, we could not expect the men to take more responsibility unless there was a corresponding increase in the extent to which they could control the system. (We believe this principle to be generally true.) We thus developed a more or less continuous chain of procedures, each chain being worked out very thoroughly with the people concerned and resulting in a very active team of workers carrying everything through.

New criteria

In preparation for Phase B of the Norwegian experiments, a good deal of theoretical work was done, both in the further development of socio-technical systems theory and in the elaboration of new criteria for job design.* In spite of the controversies among social scientists about work satisfaction, which have been mentioned, these criteria have never been seriously challenged:

First, general psychological requirements that pertain to the content of a job, its design and meaning in the larger setting were formulated. These relate to a person's day-to-day work as well as to his needs for learning and personal growth:

A the need for the content of a job to be reasonably demanding in terms other than sheer endurance, and yet to provide a minimum of variety (not necessarily novelty);

B the need for being able to learn on the job (which implies standards and knowledge of results) and to go on learning – again a question of neither too much nor too little;

C the need for some minimal area of decision-making that the individual can call his own;

D the need for some minimal degree of social support and recognition in the workplace;

E the need to be able to relate what the individual does and what he produces to his social life;

F the need to feel that the job leads to some sort of desirable future.

These requirements are obviously not confined to any one level of employment. Nor is it possible to meet them in the same way in all work settings or for all kinds of people.

These requirements, however, were too general to serve as principles for job design. They needed to be linked to the objective characteristics of industrial jobs. The result was a list of criteria as follows:

* (15), Appendix V.

36

At the level of the individual

A *Optimum variety of tasks* within the job. Too much variety can be inefficient for training and production as well as frustrating for the worker. However, too little can be conducive to boredom or fatigue. The optimum level would be that which allows the operator to take a rest from a high level of attention or effort in a demanding activity while working at another and, conversely, which allows him to stretch himself and his capacities after a period of routine activity.

B *A meaningful pattern of tasks that gives to each job a semblance of a single overall task.* The tasks should be such that – although involving different levels of attention, degrees of effort, or kinds of skill – they are interdependent: that is, the carrying out of one task makes it easier to get on with the next or gives a better end result to the overall task. Given such a pattern, the worker can help to find a method of working suitable to his requirements, and he can more easily relate his job to that of others.

C *Optimum length of work cycle.* Too short a cycle means too much finishing and starting; too long a cycle makes it difficult to build up a rhythm of work.

D *Some scope for setting standards of quantity and quality of production and a suitable feedback of knowledge of results.* Minimum standards generally have to be set by management to determine whether a worker is sufficiently trained, skilled, or careful to hold the job. Workers are more likely to accept responsibility for higher standards if they have some freedom in setting them and are more likely to learn from the job if there is feedback. They can neither effectively set standards nor learn if there is not a quick enough feedback of knowledge of results.

E *The inclusion in the job of some of the auxiliary and preparatory tasks.* The worker cannot and will not accept responsibility for matters, outside his control. In so far as the preceding criteria are met, then the inclusion of such 'boundary tasks' will extend the scope of the worker's responsibility and make for involvement in the job.

F *The tasks included in the job should include some degree of care, skill, knowledge, or effort that is worthy of respect in the community.*

G *The job should make some perceivable contribution to the utility of the product for the consumer.*

At the level of the group

H *Providing for 'interlocking' tasks, job rotation, or physical proximity where there is a necessary interdependence of jobs* (for technical or psychological reasons). At a minimum this helps to sustain communication and to create mutual understanding between workers whose tasks are inter-dependent and thus lessens friction, recriminations, and 'scapegoating'. At best, this procedure will help to create work groups that enforce standards of co-operation and mutual help.

I *Providing for interlocking tasks, job rotation, or physical proximity where the individual jobs entail a relatively high degree of stress.* Stress can arise from apparently simple things, such as physical activity, concentration, noise, or isolation, if these persist for long periods. Left to their own devices, people will become habituated, but the effects of the stress will tend to be reflected in more mistakes, accidents, and the like. Communication with others in a similar plight tends to lessen the strain.

J *Providing for interlocking tasks, job rotation, or physical proximity where the individual jobs do not make an obvious perceivable contribution to the utility of the end product.*

K *Where a number of jobs are linked together by interlocking tasks or job rotation they should as a group:*
  i have some semblance of an overall task which makes a contribution to the utility of the product;
  ii have some scope for setting standards and receiving knowledge of results;
  iii have some control over the 'boundary tasks' (i.e. tasks of a service or voluntary character).

These criteria were not intended to be final. For instance, they were developed at a time when concern for ecology and sensitivity to third-world needs was perhaps less than it is now. But it is important to understand that they are not 'merely humanitarian' in a welfare sense. They are systemic: when work roles are designed in a way that takes account of psychological and social realities, systems function better. To give a small example, from experience: in a conventional work study programme in a small hospital, it was decided that nurses should no longer take specimens from the wards to the pathology laboratory for testing. Instead a porter (on lower pay) was introduced to perform this unskilled task. As a result, the scheduling of work in the pathology laboratory got more and more out of line with the needs of the wards, and the relationships between the two departments deteriorated sharply. When it was the nurses who had taken the specimens to the laboratory technicians (overlap of roles) each had been kept aware of the other's needs and had, probably without thinking much about it, made adjustments.

New methods

These developments are not, of course, the only thing which has been happening. Another important stream of development during the last fifty years has been in the field of ergonomics. Ergonomists have, on the whole, concerned themselves with two kinds of things: defining the conditions, either in the environment or in the requirements of a task, beyond which it would be damaging to the health or beyond the capacity of the human operator; and designing tasks (in the positive sense), so that optimal use should be made of the known, or experimentally verifiable, characteristics of human operators. In this, ergonomists have tended to concern themselves with the more readily measurable and observable human characteristics, and with removing difficulties in the way of performing a task, rather than with such vague-sounding things as commitment or autonomy. They have, on the other hand, become positively involved in the design of technology and are used to collaborating with engineers in design. In the socio-technical systems work described so far, the organisation around technology has tended to be the focus of major re-design: this involves detailed analysis of technical parameters, but research workers have not, on the whole, got into the design of the technology itself. I have long felt(29) that the criteria of the social scientists and the methods of the ergonomists should be brought closer together. There is a great deal which still needs to be learned about multi-disciplinary and inter-disciplinary work.

One method to be learned from ergonomics is the systematic testing of alternatives. This was used in the re-design of Esso Petroleum Co.'s aircraft fuelling station at London Airport(41).

The situation was that, after landing, aircraft parked at any one of about 100 stands on the long-haul and short-haul 'aprons' of the airport. The turn-around time for most aircraft was about one hour, but one airline was already trying to reduce this to half an hour. In this time not only did passengers and fuel have to be loaded, but caterers, maintenance engineers, cleaners, etc. all needed to park near and work on the plane.

The job of the controller in the fuelling station was to make sure that fuelling trucks reached the aircraft on time, and the worst thing that could happen was that he should be responsible for delaying an aircraft. For information about aircraft movements the controller had the arrival and departure schedules of the airlines who were Esso customers; minute-to-minute information about the actual approach and arrival of aircraft was received by two tickertape machines from the air traffic control centre; information about the specific fuelling needs of particular aircraft was supplied by electrowriter and by telephone links with the airlines; and information about the availability of drivers and trucks, came from duty rosters and truck logs.

This job had been becoming increasingly difficult. The rate of traffic through the airport was increasing at about 15 per cent per year; traffic problems on the ground were increasing in proportion, and one could 'lose' a truck in ground traffic for up to forty minutes; and the company was very cost-conscious and kept to a minimum the controller's resources of trucks and drivers.

Criteria concerning skill and autonomy were not a problem. In interviews with the controllers, it became clear that the importance of the job was clear to all and liked by all. They were very much identified with the success of the operation and had many ideas about its improvement. But all of them, in one way or another, complained of 'stress', 'fatigue', and inability to unwind. Inevitably some informal ways of coping were being found: 'When I know I'm going to get a delay, I phone my pal who's maintenance engineer for the airline. He'll pretend there's something the matter with the engine and start pulling it to bits.'

After detailed analysis of the system, re-design suggestions were proposed and were considered in several cycles of discussions with all the controllers and supervisors who were the potential users of the system. Then a simulated control room, incorporating the new features, was built in a laboratory, and simulation experiments were designed. The programmes were written from information supplied by management, supervisors, and controllers, whose experience of the job was essential for presenting an accurate picture of the system. Questionnaires and interviews tested opinions at different stages of the experiment.

The controllers and supervisors then came and worked the simulated control room, testing and comparing four different methods of working under three different load conditions (the current load, the load predicted for the following year's peak period, and the anticipated load for five years ahead). The intention was that the people who would be operating the system could contribute their experience to its design; and they would be able to try out some ideas of the designers which were unfamiliar to them (and which they at first did not like) in safe conditions, to try a number of alternatives before deciding on a solution, and to have some idea of how long that solution would remain viable. The solution arrived at in this way was installed and, four years later, is still in use and well liked.

Simulation and the testing of alternatives are not, of course, new concepts in design; it is unusual, however, to find such explicit and realistic attention paid to the human factors in the situation. The methods can also be extended very much further to include industrial relations and motivational aspects of work design (for instance, the controllers' concern for scheduling rest-pauses and meal breaks for truck drivers emerged as an important criterion). It is quite possible to simulate some of the 'softer' aspects of social system functioning, such as the effect on a group which has inter-dependent roles when one member stays away or is slower than the others.*

Such methods are costly in their use of time and skill, but expenditure would seem to be most worthwhile before large sums are irreversibly invested. In particular, the timing of design processes would be affected. When attempts are made to include a social science contribution to design(31) it can happen that, although everyone on the design team is willing to try, time schedules do not permit the research and testing activities which the process implies. The high cost would seem to be most clearly worthwhile in the design of new technologies ('new' of course begs the question: novelty is a matter of degree, and very few situations are wholly new). If legislation is being considered, it would be worth considering the suggestion that a percentage of the cost of new

* Murray is currently working on the idea of 'socio-technical experiential learning'. See(36), p. 4, footnote.

capital projects should be spent on activities explicitly concerned with the design of the roles in the system from the point of view of the needs and characteristics of the people who will be using the system.

4. Current developments in work organisation

The development of experiments and programmes

The idea that human characteristics – not only in the sense of limiting characteristics but in the sense of emotional and developmental needs – should feature explicitly in the design of working situations spread very slowly at first. From the late 1960s onwards, however, it began to spread more rapidly, and 1973 was characterised by an explosive growth of interest, at least at the level of public discussion and the media. There is also an increasing number of professional conferences, meetings, and seminars, with some risk that the same participants keep meeting each other, while some of the better-known experiments become busy centres of scientific tourism.

The number of field experiments and programmes of change has not grown anything like as rapidly as has the amount of public discussion, but it has been growing too. There are now probably about two hundred documented case studies available. For the most part such experiments have developed at the level of individual firms and organisations, but in some instances the support, or at least the monitoring, of changes has become institutionalised at wider levels. For example, in Denmark a committee formed by the three labour market organisations within the metal industry (the labour union, the employers' association, and the foremen's association) has guided and co-ordinated experimentation in seven firms, the costs of co-ordinating activities and of evaluation research being covered by the Danish Productivity Council(1). In Great Britain, coinciding with the publication of the report 'On the Quality of Working Life'(50), a tripartite working party (Government, Trades Union Congress, and Confederation of British Industry) was set up which has been hearing evidence from firms and experts and informing itself on the subject, with a view to formulating a policy.

The country where development has been most rapid and most widespread is up to now undoubtedly Sweden. A number of reasons have been put forward to explain this rapid growth. First of all, there were factors in the labour market: during the last business peak, at the end of the 1960s, it became increasingly clear that people could not be found who were willing to undertake the lowest-level jobs in industry, and an unduly high proportion of immigrant workers were having to be placed in such jobs. Secondly, these trends coincided with the publication of the early results from the Norwegian Industrial Democracy programme, and a series of seminars held in Sweden about the Norwegian experience received wide publicity. Thirdly, surveys among school-children revealed that a very high proportion of young people in their last years at school did not want to work in industry: this confirmed to observers the idea that there was too great a disparity between the style of life and values generated by the education system and the style of life commonly experienced at work. Sweden is small enough and the process of communication rapid enough for such systemic consequences of policy to emerge clearly and to be assessed; indeed, Sweden currently forms something of a national case study.

Developments in Sweden

In Sweden, during the last few years, there has been a dramatic growth in activities connected with increased participation in public as well as in industrial life. Changes have been going on simultaneously in the education system, in local communities and public administration, and in public and private industry.

As regards work organisation, the Swedish Confederation of Trade Unions (LO) in its 1971 programme challenged management prerogatives on a wide basis, including the prerogative of deciding how work shall be done(42). The programme devotes a chapter to job satisfaction and traces the links and inconsistencies between the design of jobs and the traditions of authoritarian management and organisation in industry on the one hand, and values and styles of life in other parts of society on the other, pointing to the 'glaring differences that now show up between conditions at work and those outside the factory gates'. The Swedish Employers' Confederation (SAF) has also, to a more

limited extent, accepted the need for new forms of organisation(2).
A second large employee organisation, the Central Organisation
of Civil Servants (TCO), has joined in the debate with demands
that 'employees be guaranteed insight into and influence over
activities at all levels in the establishment'. In a joint communication from SAF, TCO, and LO in 1971, 'increased productivity
and satisfaction with work' are put forward as an objective for
locally established industrial councils.

As a result of such interest and of government support, a
number of institutions have been established to take care of the
realisation of experiments in new forms of organisation. A summary of the activities of these institutions, condensed from Hed-
berg(19), is given below:*

A The Delegation for Democracy in Administration (DEFF),
operating within the Civil Service, began by defining 'reference points for trial activities'. In a series of discussion papers,
they elaborate their views on the relationship between representation of interested parties and objectivity, the tracing of
borderlines between politics and administration, the extent of
personnel participation, etc. They have initiated trial activities
at a number of workplaces in the Civil Service. These are so far
largely concerned with employee participation in personnel
policies, recruitment, promotion, etc.

B The Development Council for State-owned Industries has five
projects. Reports have been published on a tobacco company,
a shipyard, and a restaurant company. The reports contain suggestions, which are now being implemented, for changes in work
organisation and for the setting up of consultative procedures.

C In local government there are some activities involving education, planning, and medical services.

D The Co-operative Union and Wholesale Society is at present
engaged in two trial activities.

E The Development Council for Matters of Co-operation (UR),
which is concerned with the private sector, has formed a special
working group for research (URAF), the research secretariat of
which is located at the Swedish Council for Personnel Administration (PA Council). Together with research scientists at
various academic institutions, URAF has planned and initiated

* See also (2).

45

a research programme in order to study what factors promote or hinder the process of democratisation. The programme currently consists of nine major long-term studies. They cover changes in working processes and work organisation; changes in the role of management (both the design of management roles and the selection of supervisors); efforts to bring employee influence to bear on the formation of personnel policy and to widen the influence of employees within the representative system; and changes in office procedures.

F The technical department of the Swedish Employers' Confederation has made its resources available to member companies, where management and employees have co-operated in various forms of re-organisation. Some ten case reports are in process of publication.

G A large number of experiments are developing spontaneously without outside help. A survey conducted in the summer of 1973 by the Employers' Confederation brought to light some five hundred firms which said they were doing something in this direction.

As has been suggested, some of the systemic implications of all this activity are becoming apparent already. For instance, people monitoring industrial experiments are critical of some of the original theories on which they were based and are working to use the outcomes of experiments for further theoretical and conceptual development. At university level one large engineering school makes it compulsory for all engineers to learn some ergonomics and industrial psychology, while plans for the new technical university at Luleå include substantial blocks of behavioural science teaching for technologists.

Results of experiments and programmes

The evaluation of complex changes presents serious methodological problems. For one thing, the changes need to be evaluated in terms of the aims – which may vary considerably – of those who initiate them. Some programmes have as their aim the solution of a specific problem or symptom, such as recruitment or absenteeism; in some programmes, productivity measures feature largely, at least as limiting conditions; while in some, the interest, excitement, and idealism of the experiment itself is the mainspring and sufficient justification, while productivity losses are thought worth bearing and improvements considered as unexpected bonuses. Secondly, 'those who initiate' experiments may not be easy to identify, since there may be differences between the aims of different parties in a situation. Thirdly, there are usually a number of changes going on at the same time, not all of which form part of the experiment.

Detailed evaluation may therefore be as complicated and expensive an exercise, and require as much expertise, as the experiments which are being reviewed. If carried out on any large and systematic scale, it brings additional problems of possible interference with the original experiment. Finally, cynics can always raise the unanswerable question of objectivity which is created by the relationship between evaluator and evaluated: if they are the same person or group, they may be thought to be biassed, wanting the experiment to appear in a favourable light; if they are different persons or groups, the evaluators may be influenced by separate aims of their own.

Quantitative and systematic evaluation

Quantitative

When it comes to giving quantitative results of experiments, another point needs to be made. Some of the pressure to demonstrate results in productivity terms seems to show anxiety about the nature of what is being attempted rather than about productivity itself. It is doubtful whether any 'total, integrated Management Information System' has ever had to prove itself under such detailed and costly scrutiny as is required of some of these programmes. In turn, such pressure can lead to rather unconvincing simplistic success stories, which a Dutchman called the 'Hallelujah stories' and a Swede the 'Smörgåsbord accounts'. Hopefully, one can begin to detect a move away from Hallelujah stories, towards more realistic and less defensive accounts of what actually happens. Such accounts are more likely to appear in a climate of genuine interest in outcomes, whatever they are, and willingness to learn from them, rather than one of 'prove yourself if you can!'

With these reservations, here nevertheless are some quantitative results from the report *Work in America* (53), which was completed in 1972:

AT&T: 'absenteeism decreased from 2% to 1.4%. Turnover practically eliminated'.

Bell System: 'Turnover decreased by 9.3% in the experimental group and increased 13.1% in the control group. Overtime hours decreased about 50%'.

Texas Instruments: 'assembly time per unit decreased from 138 to 32 hours. Absenteeism, turnover, leaving time, complaints and trips to health center decreased'.

Nobø Fabrikker A/S, Norway: 'In the one-year experiment, production rates increased 22% and hourly earnings increased 11%'.

ICI, Gloucester, England: '20% reduction in labor, 20% increase in production, 25% increase in pay, and a 30% cut in supervision'.

PPG Industries, Lexington, North Carolina: 'Productivity increased by 12% over the previous two years'.

Monsanto, Electronics Division, New Jersey: 'Turnover, which had been high among unskilled jobs, averaged 6% annually in the five years of the program'.

Monsanto, Textile Division, Florida: 'Waste loss dropped to zero, operators monitor 50% more instruments and half of the old supervisors not needed'.

Syntex, Mexico and California: 'Volume sales in the two experimental groups increased by 116% and 20% over the control groups'.

Monsanto, Agriculture Division, Iowa: 'Production increased 75% in the four months after the change'.

Oldsmobile Division of General Motors, Lansing, Michigan: 'Absenteeism decreased 6% in engineering and 6.5% in assembly – while rising 11% in the rest of Oldsmobile. There were "improved product quality...and reduced costs"'.

Corning Glass Works, Medfield, Massachusetts: 'In the six months after the change, rejects dropped from 23% to 1% and absenteeism from 8% to 1%'.

Alcan Aluminum, Oswego, New York: 'Absenteeism decreased to about 2.5% compared to an industry average of about 10%. Productivity increased'.

Micro-Wax Dept., Shell Stanlow Refinery, Ellesmere Port, England: '"Output" in three sections increased by 35%,

40%, and 100% over 1965. Absence and sickness decreased from 4.3% in 1963 to 3.3% in 1969'.

Philips Electrical Industries, Holland: 'By 1967, waste and repairs decreased by 4%...unspecified savings of lower managerial personnel'.

Ferado Company, England: 'less turnover...original delivery times have been cut by seven-eighths'.

Netherlands PTT: '15% increase in output per man-hour'.

Kaiser Aluminum, West Virginia: 'Tardiness is now "non-existent". Maintenance costs are down 5.5%. Maintenance work is done with more "quality"'.

Systematic

The nearest thing to a systematic across-the-board evaluation is a *Survey of Some Western European Experiments in Motivation* which was carried out in 1970 – a little ahead of the present wave of interest – by Alan Wilkinson of ICI Ltd(49).

He used a travelling fellowship award in order to try to locate and visit companies in Europe which were at that time experimenting in this field, and to assess what results they were achieving. It is the only systematic attempt of this kind which is at the moment available.

There are obvious problems of defining what constitutes an 'experiment in motivation', but Wilkinson meant, in general, experiments which were concerned with the content of work. He managed to locate thirty-five separate experiments, within twenty-five companies, in Norway, Denmark, Sweden, the Netherlands, and the United Kingdom. He visited twenty-five of those experiments at first hand, and the other ten were reported to him by people who were informed about them or who had taken part in them. On closer examination, he rejected three experiments as not being relevant, and a further eleven had been started too recently for him to form any opinion on the degree of success or the results achieved. There remained twenty-one applications which he considered both relevant to the survey and sufficiently established to enable some judgement to be formed as to their sucess or failure. The following are extracts from his report on them:

The most notable feature of the attempt to collect measures of success or failure was an almost universal absence of 'hard' measurement! While many companies were convinced that the experiments had led to improvements in productivity of some kind, there was scant evidence that anyone had set out from the beginning of the experiment to monitor the effects of these changes.

Of course, there is the problem of separating the effect of these changes from the effect of other inputs; but few companies have even made the attempt. When questioned about this curious lack of interest in monitoring experiments, several contacts answered as follows:

A 'We do not regard this primarily as a productivity improvement technique, but rather as a change which is essential if industry is to survive in the environment of the future, with its increasing Welfare State benefits, with increasing social pressures for greater involvement in decisions which affect the life of the individual, with growing political and union pressures for "industrial democracy", with the changing methods of education and expectations from life which these are engendering in the student etc.'
(Even in these cases, it was generally thought that increased productivity should arise, albeit as a secondary benefit, if the experiment was successful.)

B 'There is little point in monitoring the effects of such an experiment, since even if the results are not as expected, it is impossible to revert to the former situation . . . '

Despite the dearth of hard measurement, there were nevertheless 14 out of the 21 'experienced' experiments where the contacts left the author with the conviction that there had been some increase in productivity as a direct result of the experiment. The term Productivity Increase is here used fairly broadly to mean anything which has contributed towards an increase in the ratio of profits to costs. The 14 companies exhibit several different kinds of productivity improvement; in some cases, there has been a reduction in manning while output and quality were maintained; in others, there has been an increase in output or sales for a constant labour cost; in others, the saving has been in administrative and other indirect costs; in yet others, there have been significant cost reductions in the area of waste raw materials or reject finished products; and so on. These 14 companies will be henceforth referred to in this report as 'successful applications'.

Of the remaining seven companies, two quoted what amounted to a *loss* (that is, a fall in the ratio of profits to costs); the other five were unable to offer any convincing evidence that the exercise had in any way been worthwhile, other than in some cases a rather optimistic-sounding view that 'attitudes have improved'. These seven companies are referred to elsewhere in the report as 'non-successful applications'. They are deliberately not referred to as 'failures' because the criteria of success which are used are not necessarily the criteria for the managers concerned in the experiments.

For example, in one Dutch company (in fact, one of the two mentioned above which suffered a loss) there was an apparently sincere view that the company had never set out with any intention of improving productivity; they had simply been trying to keep in step with a changing environment, in order to ensure their survival in the long term. They admitted having made losses, but argued very convincingly that there was no knowing how much worse the losses might have been had they not taken these steps. It is obvious that a firm which embarks on an application . . . with this kind of philosophy cannot be termed a failure if they do not achieve results which they were not aiming for in the first place; and several companies like this were encountered both in the 'experienced' and 'inexperienced' applications, though not all were as lucid in defence of their philosophy as the rather extreme example quoted above. . .

What initiates an exercise of this kind?

. . . It is perhaps significant to note that when the successful applications were ranked in descending order of degrees of success – which, of course, remembering the absence of hard measures, is a fairly subjective process – four out of the first seven applications were initiated not as experiments in motivation, but as fairly conventional productivity improvement exercises which attempted to take into account not only the technical aspects of the business but also the most recent thinking on how the human resource should be handled.

This difference in emphasis seems to have important consequences; less is required in the way of changing management attitudes as a precursor, since from the beginning the exercise is

51

oriented towards goals which are the traditional goals of management; the forecast benefits require much less 'faith' than is the case in a 'pure' motivational job structuring exercise, and the general feeling generated is far more one of evolution than one of revolution or novelty. . . There was quite a lot of evidence gathered on the survey to confirm the view that to attempt too much change too quickly, or to attempt to change too many things at once (for example, attitudes, job structures, organization, and payment systems simultaneously) was to invite a costly failure. . .

. . . in several of the experiments surveyed one of the main factors initiating the exercise was some particular stimulus which came not so much from within the work group concerned as from the environment.

Opportunism

In ten of the 32 applications included in this survey, the impression gained was that the main stimulus to beginning an experiment of this kind was a change in environmental circumstances which management recognized as an opportunity to attempt to bring the company/department 'up to date' in terms of job design and organization structure.

One example of this [occurred in a] Dutch banking company, where the stimulus to change was the opportunity provided by the merger of two companies, creating a secondary set of circumstances in which management saw opportunities for improvement – namely, an empty office arose in a provincial town as a result of this merger; in this area there was no acute labour shortage as there had been in the cities; owing to Government policy on building grants in this particular area (which was land newly reclaimed from the sea) it was seen that future expansion in this area would be very cheap. . .

Another example of management grasping at opportunities to initiate change of this sort was found on a much smaller scale. . . in one of the design offices of a company where change had been talked about over a long period as part of a Management by Objectives programme. The opportunity arose in the form of a change of chief supervisor in the design office. It was recognised that the new man, who was much younger than the previous incumbent, might be more receptive to ideas which had been talked about for a long time, and this indeed proved to be the case.

This exemplifies several of the experiments included in the survey, in that even where the need to change has been agreed and a decision made to proceed, actually making a start has been delayed until an opportunity presented itself. The timing of change is an extremely important aspect. . .

Significant union influence

It does of course go without saying that, in the majority of the examples used, trades unions, or employees' organizations, have played a part at some stage in the application. In seven of the 32 cases, however, the influence of employee representative organizations was one of the significant factors in actually triggering off and planning the details of the experiment. . .

Special influence of new plant

In at least four cases, the major factor which led management to consider the application of new ways of handling the human resource was the fact that an organization and a set of jobs had to be devised for a new factory or plant.

Dissatisfactions with traditional organizations and jobs, coupled perhaps with a knowledge of the new theories (from reading about them in trade magazines, hearing them discussed on television etc.) led to a decision to attempt to find alternative job and organization structures rather than simply to install carbon copies of previous systems. . .

Preparatory investigation and training

Most companies included in the survey felt the need, having once made the decision to get involved in a motivation exercise, or a change which took account of motivational ideas, to gather data of some kind about the company and its employees which could be used as a basis for redesigning jobs and organization. In addition, many companies felt that some preparation of people in the organization – either management or workers or both – was needed. . .

Analysis of the technical system

Twenty-one of the applications included a thorough investigation into the technical system concerned. Generally this involved taking a fresh look at the machinery, methods and raw materials, by beginning with the question, 'What is the real objective of the system?' This was followed by postulating various alternative means by which this objective could be achieved, and selecting from these alternatives those which were thought to have the most chance of success, not only from the technical viewpoint, but also from the viewpoint of their motivational aspects – that is, the alternatives were evaluated both in terms of cost, level of output etc. and also in terms of opportunities for personal satisfaction, decision-making, growth and learning etc.

A typical example of this kind of analysis of the technical system is [a] Swedish plumbing organization . . . By taking a fresh look at the objective of the repair and service company, and generating alternative methods of achieving this objective, a new socio-technical system was devised which was very different from the traditional form. Where previously the repair man travelled by bicycle or tram carrying only a small bag of tools, he now travels by means of a van which is equipped as a mobile workshop/ stores. Where previously the customer had no idea of the cost of a job until the elapsed time taken to carry out the repair was known, the vast majority of the repair and service work is now contained in a fixed price list. Examples of motivational aspects which have been included in these new arrangements are such things as each repair man keeping his own special van in which he lays out his tools and stocks of spare parts as he wishes; and having received a list of orders for the day, in planning his own day's work, taking into account customers' stated preferences as to timing, and rearranging his plan as unexpected difficulties arise, or as he receives radio messages about urgent jobs.

One especially important aspect of analysing and redesigning the technical system is that concerned with 'buffer storages'. The theory is that an individual or a group can only achieve a high degree of autonomy if they are to a large extent independent, in terms of pace of working and results achieved, of other individuals or groups. To put it another way, it is difficult to have a motivated job on a traditional assembly line where the speed of working is determined by the speed of the incoming work pieces from the previous station on the line; and where the finished article or sub-assembly has had 16 or 20 people contributing to its quality.

In seven cases in this survey, it was found with careful analysis of the technical system that work could be so arranged that the individual or the small group drew its work pieces from a buffer storage, and placed its 'finished' pieces into another storage, thus achieving considerable scope for self-determination of pace. To work from a storage to a storage also has the important advantage that the piece can always be *tested* at each storage point; this means that the worker (or the small group) can know with confidence how well he is achieving against the standard existing at the time. To seek clear subsystem boundaries in this way – with a storage at either side of the subsystem and with some means of measuring and testing the work at each storage point – seems to be an important motivational technique...

The means of achieving this are various: in one example, it was achieved by rearranging work so that all the skills and effort required to make a complete piece from stores of parts were available within a small group, the responsibility for maintaining stock levels and checking the quality of the finished article also residing within the group. (Previously the production people had been dependent for stocks on people outside the group, certain operations which could affect quality had also been done outside the group, and inspection and testing was not carried out until a later stage, by which time other groups had handled the product.)

A very different way of achieving the same result was found in another example where workers operated as individuals, remaining static while the work piece passed to and from them on moving belts. Here a most intricate system of remote controlled belts and gates had been designed which enabled the worker to send for another work piece from stock when she needed it, and to send the finished piece back to stock until it was 'sent for' by the girl who carried out the subsequent operation on that piece.

This meant that the girls could choose their own pace, that they tested their own work before returning it to stock, and that they were responsible for maintaining their own substores for spare parts; when a girl decided, for example, that she was running short of a particular type of screw she had a means of signalling to the remote store to 'send for' another box of the screws, which would then be directed via the intricate series of belts and gates to her work place...

55

Analysis of the social system

In seven of the companies included in the survey, one of the initial steps in the exercise consisted of attempting to define and analyse the system from the viewpoint of how best to satisfy social needs. This means that, in addition to looking at the technical system to see where it was failing to fulfil the human needs (e.g. uncovering situations where individuals were required to work on rapid repetitive jobs with little or no contact with anyone else, a situation which leads to stress and nervous complaints), steps were taken to discover the *special* needs, attitudes and relationships which existed among the people who worked in the section being studied. To use such an approach is difficult for even small groups of people and impossible to apply to large numbers. It goes a step further than making the general assumptions about the *average* person which result from Herzberg's and Maslow's theories; it recognises that the individual or the group may not be 'average', and seeks to find out more accurate information about the special needs and problems of that individual or that group.

Various means of doing this were used, but essentially in all seven cases this amounted to asking the people concerned to state their preferences and problems. A typical example is from a Danish paint and ink company where, for six months prior to the author's visit, groups of employees had been having regular dicussions at which they were encouraged to talk about their problems and their needs. In this company there was recognition on the part of senior management that feelings as well as facts were important in the design of work organization...

...Analysis of the social system, if it is to be more than mere lip service, should result in jobs and organization structures which to some extent are 'tailor-made' for the individuals and group in question. This means something more than designing jobs and organizations against a general theory of motivation and human needs. It means designing jobs and organization against quite specific needs... This leads to situations which may well offend the sensibilities of many of today's managers who, since the words 'scientific management' were first coined, have tended more and more to prefer the tidy solution, the neat model of the work situation. Indeed, work study people have been the prime movers in guiding managers in this direction.

56

To give examples of what is meant by 'a tailor-made job/ organization', consider the following:

A [A] Norwegian chemical company, where on one manufacturing plant there are four shifts, all of whom operate the same technical process with the same objective. There is a different group structure on each shift; the number of personnel differs from shift to shift (not as a result of any temporary shortage of labour, but from group preference); on each shift there is a supervisor, but he plays a very different role on one shift to the role of the supervisor on another shift – for example, one supervisor acts as a technical consultant, another as a sort of shift personnel officer. The author was told during his visit that one of these shift supervisors had recently approached his superior and told him that he felt that his particular shift could now operate without any shift supervision at all...

B Another example...comes from a Danish company manufacturing high quality electrical and electronic consumer goods. Here,...in some cases groups were given the responsibility of democratically deciding the make-up of the group – in other words, they as a group decided whether a particular individual should be accepted into the group, or conversely whether one of the existing members was so unsuitable as to be expelled from the group...

C In a small factory in Sweden manufacturing building materials, discussion of the preferences of individuals and of the working group led to the design and installation of a unique and very complex shift system with the following sequence:

7 nights
5 afternoons
2 off
7 mornings
7 off
5 afternoons
2 off
5 mornings
2 off

Each man worked this rota over a six week period. Every shift consisted of two five-man teams, except for the night shift, which only required one five-man team, and the weekends on which one five-man team worked a 12-hour morning shift and another worked a 12-hour afternoon shift. The system included an allowance for a handover overlap. The main reason for the group preferring such a system was that each man had five out of six weekends off and one full week off out of every six. This is not a tidy solution, nor is it a solution which management would be likely to have designed 'scientifically'.

Analysis of the information system

A feature which was found to some degree in 20 of the applications included in the survey (10 of them belong to the group of 14 'successful applications') was a careful analysis and some re-design of the information systems in which the work group concerned were involved. This seems to be one of the most important aspects of designing jobs and organization from the motivational as well as the efficiency viewpoint...

Management style and attitude

'Involve' or 'Consult'... at the initial stage of changes

On seven occasions, the author was told that all employees affected, down to the lowest level, had been 'involved/consulted' at the design stage for new machinery or plant. In every case, the people concerned were extremely enthusiastic about the results achieved, both in terms of efficient technical design and the commitment of the people involved towards making the new machinery work.

A typical example was found in a Dutch plywood plant, where workers were involved in the design of a new crane. In this particular example, the design had largely been completed when it was decided to ask for the opinions of the people who would operate and use the crane. When their views on the design were made known, the flaws detected in the original design were so serious that major changes had to be made. It was estimated that approximately £2,000 had been saved by canvassing the views of those who would be asked to operate the new machinery *before* construction began.

The results of this kind of involvement were very similar in the other six cases where it was found.

Regular production-oriented meetings

In 11 cases, an important aspect in the job restructuring experiment was the institution of regular meetings which included the manager, the supervisors and the workers, and which had as their objective the identification and solving of day-to-day problems concerning production. (Many companies of course have regular meetings between management and workers; however, these often in practice turn out to be 'selling sessions' for management ideas, or a forum for grumbles about 'hygiene' problems.)

A representative example of the kind of meeting referred to here is the 'morning meeting' instituted at the Norwegian chemical company. These are a daily routine, and include one or two of the operators and maintenance workers as well as the managers and supervisors. The workers have a rota for attending the meetings, which concentrate on matters concerning production. An important feature is that all decisions taken are documented; the action agreed upon is recorded; and the name of the person responsible for ensuring that such action is taken is also recorded. These documents are widely circulated, and awkward questions asked if agreed action has not been taken by the specified date...

Involvement of all concerned in project teams

In five of the applications seen, an important aspect of the reorganization was the introduction of a policy of involving representatives of all levels concerned, in 'project teams'. By a 'project team' is meant a team which is set up with a particular commission to solve a particular problem (a rather different system from the regular forum described above). The advantages of such a procedure from the viewpoint of effectiveness are that the make-up of the team can be determined by the nature of the problem rather than being determined by hierarchical or departmental constraints; the advantage from the motivational viewpoint is that it provides an opportunity for showing *recognition* – i.e. recognition that each individual has something of value to offer from his own knowledge and experience in the area of problem-solving and development, in addition to being able simply to carry out routine day-to-day work.

A typical example was the Danish paint and ink company, where the senior management were so impressed with the results of this 'project team' approach, both in terms of effective problem solving and in terms of improving communication and relationships between organizationally separate groups, that they were making every effort to extend its use . . .

Management attitudes

. . . Since the theory of motivation is so emphatic that real motivation depends on the design of the job, it is to be expected that an important attitude affecting an experiment is the attitude of management towards changing jobs. This was indeed found to be the case: in 13 of the applications, there was abundant evidence that managers at high levels were willing to experiment with the design of work; nine of these 13 were 'successful' applications, and only one was a 'non-successful' application.

To illustrate this, compare [a] Dutch banking company (where jobs were altered to such an extent that the same objectives could be achieved by inexperienced, poorly qualified young girls as had previously been achieved by highly qualified specialist staff) with [a] Danish company manufacturing high quality electrical and electronic consumer goods (where there had been expensive training programmes, changes in payment systems, widespread discussion of motivation theories, attitude surveys, and all the other trappings of a sincere attempt to apply the new theories – with one exception. At this company there was a detectable unwillingness on the part of managers at several levels to alter the work itself. When questioned about this, the kind of answer they gave was 'Yes – but these people are only capable of so much'; 'Yes – but this is expensive machinery which is being handled'; 'Yes – but think of all the wasted cost of training if they don't stay long with the company', etc.). In the former case, an undisputable success had been achieved, by whatever criteria 'success' was being measured. In the latter, although a number of experiments had been going on for almost a year, there was no real evidence of any outcome which could be termed 'success'. The willingness on the part of management to alter jobs is really a symptom of the overall attitude to risk-taking . . .

The Dutch bank provides an anecdote which illustrates exactly the kind of attitude to risk-taking which is necessary for this kind of experiment to have any more than very limited success. A short time before this company was visited, there had been a mistake made by one of the girl employees, in that she omitted to photocopy a cheque. This mistake cost the company £2,000, and potentially could have cost very much more. In order to prevent this happening again, the girl's immediate supervisor wanted to install a checking procedure; however, higher management turned down this suggestion on the grounds that to behave in this way was to set foot on a path which would lead all the way back to the traditional . . . organization and job structures which had been the norm before the experiment which was triggered off by the merger.

The matter was dealt with by talking to all the girls concerned with this part of the business, telling them about the mistake, and the cost. They were also told of the decision not to install any checking procedure, being left with the thought that, as before, they were the ones responsible, and that responsibility was not going to be taken from them . . .

Commitment of top management

In 15 of the applications, when asked what was the most important single feature required for success in an experiment of this kind, the companies replied, 'Real commitment and understanding on the part of top management' . . . Commitment here means what it says: to allow experiments to take place or to engage behavioural science consultant effort because to do so is fashionable is *not* commitment . . .

In most of the 'successful' applications, it was very apparent that there was a figurehead, a leader whose personal commitment and example had inspired the people involved in the exercise. This leader, to be effective, must be sufficiently high in the organization to *act* on his beliefs. In several of the non-successful applications it was apparent that, although certain individuals were highly committed, and had been directed to plan and progress the training programmes, discussion sessions etc, they had *not* been given the authority to implement changes; when changes were proposed, the proposals had to be sent up the line, where in many cases they were turned down by managers who had not been involved in the discussions and who had little understanding or enthusiasm for what was happening. This situation is experienced at the lower levels as a feeling that top management do not really believe in the involvement and enrichment being talked about at the lower levels, and that what is happening must be some subtle manipulative plan, the real purpose of which is being concealed.

When asked to identify the most important factors contributing to the outcome of their experiment, seven of the 14 'successful' applications quoted the leadership and commitment of top management, and three of the seven 'non-successes' referred to lack of it.

Many examples of lack of management commitment were quoted (or directly exhibited) during the survey; the most common were:

A To avoid changing repetitive, 'mindless' jobs by self-delusion that the particular people in those jobs preferred that kind of work...

B Senior people to avoid taking part in training and discussion, using the excuse that they are too busy, or (less overtly) that it is not *they* who need such training.

C A fall-off in the 'push' towards job and organization change when the environmental situation changes. (For example, in one company the approach was widely adopted with a view to solving problems of high labour turnover; then came a recession, labour turnover dropped, and management interest in many parts of the company faded.)

D A re-introduction of supervision, or checking procedures, on the first occasion when an employee makes a mistake in the course of carrying out his newly enriched job...

Results of applications

The 'initial dip' phenomenon

In a number of the applications surveyed, a 'results curve' something like [the illustration] was experienced.

In other words, work and organization restructuring does not normally show an immediate improvement at the start of an experiment. What is likely is that there will be an initial *drop* in productivity while people learn their new jobs, particularly as they learn to shoulder their increased responsibilities. Part of the initial dip will be caused simply by the slowness and double-checking which anyone who is doing a new job will exhibit; part will also be caused by actual mistakes being made. It is important

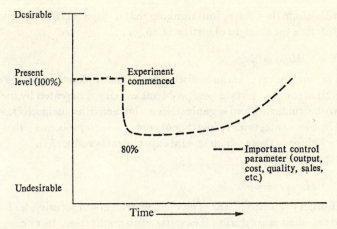

that management should expect such occurrences as part of the natural learning process, and not react by progressively removing each bit of newly given responsibility.

This 'initial dip' phenomenon is apparently common enough for the Board of one of the major companies widely involved in work design to direct its managers to *include* such a dip and its associated cost in their financial forecasts when beginning an experiment...

'Two bites at the cherry'

Another common experience, shared by six of the applications in the survey – five of them 'successes' – was that it took two distinct attempts to reach the desired change. (An example has been quoted of the Swedish purchasing department, where the first reorganization achieved the desired economic goals but failed to satisfy the human objective; after involvement of the people concerned, yet another organization structure was devised which could satisfy *all* the criteria for success.)

Although such a method – design a change, implement for a test period, then further improve it to 'iron out the bugs' – is a common enough procedure in many technical fields, it is not so widely practised in the field of man management. Too often, if a first experiment is unsuccessful, the whole thinking behind the experiment is assumed to be wrong, and every attempt is made to revert to the previous status quo. Alternatively, the effort required to make the first change has been so great that all concerned

63

will delude themselves into thinking that it was a success, rather than face the thought of further change . . .

New problems arising

The final group of features discovered in the application surveyed is an account of certain new problems which were created by the work structuring and organization design activities themselves. The three categories below do not cover all such problems – they include only those which several experiments produced in common.

Human problems

Human problems of fear of change, worries about security, and so on, often arose during the course of an application. In 11 cases, those interviewed felt that they still had some such problems, and had found no satisfactory solution. In these cases, the main problem was one of how to deal with surplus people – usually at the supervisor level.

Compulsory redundancy, or 'early retirement', was generally used as a last resort. The usual ways of reducing numbers of people were: by 'natural wastage' (although it is as well to note that job restructuring can *lower* turnover, and so forecasts of 'wastage' levels may be inaccurate); by transfer to other jobs within the company where there was a shortage; by employing surplus people as instructors in the heavy training period immediately following agreement to change job boundaries (this of course is temporary, but lasts long enough to give 'natural wastage' more time to alleviate the problem).

Although ways were generally found of avoiding dismissal, it was found in many cases that transfer to another job was almost equally unacceptable, being regarded in the eyes of those involved (if not in the eyes of management) as demotion or 'putting out to grass'.

An associated problem was the reduction of opportunities for promotion which resulted from the disappearance of one or more levels in the hierarchy. A promising approach to this problem seemed to be the 'paying-people-for-what-they-know' method . . ., where opportunities for promotion from one payment grade to the next existed *within* the work group, depending on what proportion of the total group task the individual managed to learn.

64

Demands on time

In nine cases, it was found that the preparation, design and implementation of the changes took up many more man-hours (at all levels) than had been expected. This unforeseen drain on resources had two main causes:

A Where a participative style was being attempted, the time taken to reach 'consensus' agreement on the details of a change was much longer that it would have taken to begin implementing a change operating under a 'Tell' or 'Sell' or 'Consult' style. This excessive time usage no doubt stems in part from the inexperience of all concerned in operating in a participative way; but there is no doubt, even in the few situations where small groups had become familiar with this method of decision making, that the price of commitment was time.

B In some cases (again, those in which there was a greater degree of involvement of lower levels in the design of the change) the 'technical' training load (i.e. training workers in those parts of the job which formerly they had not done) had also been under-estimated in the earlier plans.

Payment problems

In seven cases, the new job boundaries and organization had created payment problems. These were different in detail one from another, but can be described by this generalisation: the old payment system, which was retained, did not fit the new jobs and organization; and there was some powerful force at work which prevented the payment system being changed, in spite of the pressures following the organizational changes.

An example to illustrate what is meant can be taken from the Dutch plywood and timber products company. Here, before the changes, a job evaluation scheme had been used. Following the motivation experiments, it was found that, for a large proportion of the workers, jobs had been so changed that re-evaluation should have taken place (the old job evaluation scale remaining unchanged). However, the company's financial policy prevented the enriched jobs from being re-graded, which at the time of the author's visit was beginning to cause worry.

Qualitative evaluation

It will have become clear already that, whereas quantitative

65

evaluation can be used to make the case for or against undertaking or continuing an experiment or a programme of change, it is the qualitative and descriptive case studies which lead to greater understanding of the processes and problems involved. The greater the detail, and the greater the readiness to allow difficult parts of a story to be known, the greater is the learning that will take place. Here is one episode, from one experiment, as described to me by the foreman involved – it is another instance of Wilkinson's 'initial dip' phenomenon of a drop in productivity during the early phases:

Eleven girls out of a group of twenty-five had volunteered to take part in an experiment to re-structure the way in which small, high-precision electrical components were assembled. The first cost was, therefore, duplicate machinery to enable this group to work independently of the others. As with all new equipment, there were mechanical and electrical problems which caused a great deal of frustration and took several weeks to sort out. A week before the experiment began the girls had, in discussion and with the foreman as adviser, decided on the layout of the machines, but they found in practice that the layout had to be changed. From the first day they moved around between jobs and found this very difficult, particularly as the machines were new.

The foreman himself found his new role strange, since he was still also in charge of the rest of the department which continued the old style of working. 'On any other unit I'd say what I wanted; with this team I didn't, I wanted it to come from them'.

They had arranged to collect and see their own performance figures each week, and grew discouraged when these were poor.

They had been going for about five or six weeks when the first blow came. One of the girls left (for personal reasons). It threw us a lot. She was one of the highest performers on a particularly short-cycle job. She could do about 1300 of the day's output of 1500, and no-one else was as good. The team had to decide whether to run as a ten-operator team, or to try to attract one of the existing operators in from another group, or to bring in a brand new operator. They were very frustrated, their performance had not been good, the others in the department were laughing

at them and they could not attract anyone in. But they were
finding it very difficult to balance with only ten and they decided
to take a brand new girl.

Then came another body-blow. The one they chose (from the
training school) was not very good. She did struggle but she was
only average. She was not the one I would have picked but if I
ruled against them we would have got into a situation where the
experiment folded up. I had to hold myself back . . .

One of the main problems we had in the early stages was that
they were trying hard as individuals but it wasn't blending. Some
tried to emerge as leader and I had to keep stressing that nobody
was more important than anyone else. If I was on the floor and
went to speak to one of them I made a point of not speaking to
the same person on two occasions running . . .

There was a drop in performance at week 20 because we took
them all to the feeder factory to meet the people who make the
components. Now if they have a problem they get in touch with
them direct and they can put a face to the voice . . .

In the sixth month we got up to the factory level of performance
and there was more training going on in that time than ever in
any other. Even with all that training we got to just above the
factory level. Quality is now above the factory level . . .

Turnover was halved over the first twelve months . . .
Absenteeism in the rest of the factory came down from 17 per cent
to 13 per cent (there were labour market changes) ; in this team
it came down to 8 per cent. We are running with lower stock
levels than before because when people can move about you can
do with less stock than when they stay at one job . . .

We now have two more teams working on the same principle
and another one starting next month. They all came and
volunteered . . .

We have never had quite the same starting problems again . . .
the first group took all the buffeting . . .

They have worked out a way of recruiting new members
when it becomes necessary, in collaboration with the instructress
in the training school . . .

The secondary jobs that a 'co-ordinator' used to do, the
paper-work and the recording, they do it themselves. They
deliver the forms into the correct places, to stores, to stock-control,
etc., and they do the monitoring themselves . . .

Long-term evaluation

One more evaluation will be reported, because it concerns the longest-standing experiments, those carried out by Rice in Ahmedabad. In 1970 two members of the Tavistock Institute, Miller and Shaw, visited the Calico Mills for a follow-up study. Broadly speaking, what was being called the 'group system' now encompassed several widely different systems of working. In the experimental automatic loom shed (still called 'experimental' after seventeen years) the new work organisation and the productivity improvements had been sustained with great success. Group identification was high; members of the groups cooperated with one another in their work; the group leader exercised a boundary function; supervisors respected this function and seldom intervened; norms of performance had persisted. In a second shed ('Calico Auto') a discrepant system had evolved, and, in two more, systems which appeared to be intermediate between the two.

Miller explains these developments in terms of interaction with the environment.* As the company enhanced its reputation for design and quality in the Indian markets, so its management aspired to becoming increasingly competitive in exports, not only within the relatively less developed markets of the Far East, the Middle East, and Africa, but also in the more stringent markets of the West. The products of 'Calico Auto' were most affected by these new aspirations, with constantly increasing pressure to extract the finest yarn possible out of each grade of cotton available, leading to increased probability of breaking and therefore increased amounts of preventive and corrective attention required, as well as other problems.

The method of working had been designed so that each group had a certain amount of resilience to absorb and adjust to variations, mainly through flexibility. Reversion to more rigid differentiation of labour might in fact be a symptom that the group had exceeded the limits of its capacity to adjust to external change. In the course of the initial experiments, top management had withdrawn its attention from the sheds, since everything was going well. The supervisors appear not to have been sufficiently trained in the new theories and were in some cases new. When things

* These notes are over-simplified. E. J. Miller's follow-up study appears in *Human Relations*, 28 (1975), 349–86.

became difficult, instead of (a) trying to reduce the source of the disturbance, i.e. managing the boundaries of the work system, and (b) trying to increase the resilience of the group, they reverted to direct intervention in the work of the groups and therefore further helped to decrease their flexibility and resilience. Miller concluded that further support and training for the new culture was needed.

5. Discussion – The next generation of issues

Work design in context

Work plays such an important part in the life of individuals and of society that changing the nature of work implies nothing less than a culture change. The difficulty of making such a change lies in the fact that individuals have made adjustments to the earlier situation, and institutions have grown up to deal with it. Therefore, while there are indeed a large number of experiments now taking place, nowhere has critical mass been achieved. The culture change is a new and tender plant, and it is quite possible that in a difficult economic climate some change programmes may be postponed or discontinued. At a time when economic problems are again beginning to loom large, questions may well be asked about the degree of priority, or even the relevance, of changes such as the ones that have been described.

The experiments which falter are likely to be those which are not yet well rooted, or which were only undertaken for reasons of fashion. Those which continue developing in a difficult situation are also likely to be of two kinds: those that have already given their organisations a new kind of flexibility and resilience, and those which are in any case congruent with their environment.

In the long run these change programmes will exert influences of their own and may themselves lead to new institutions, organisational forms, and technologies. They should lead to a greater interpenetration of boundaries between industry and the rest of society, lessening the split between the values expressed in the working arrangements of society and the values expressed in its other institutions. Nevertheless, there has to be some congruence between these experiments and their environment. They have to make sense in the economic context (in that they do not lead to bankruptcy), in the technological context (in that they are feasible), in the industrial relations context, and in the organisational context. These latter two will be discussed in a little more detail.

The industrial relations context

As Delamotte puts it, 'Union attitudes to the quality of working life may differ from one country to another, within a country from one enterprise to another, and even within an enterprise from one plant to another. Within a workers' federation, positions taken at the top towards the idea may not be reflected in positions taken by a local union, confronted with practical changes'(12).

The amount and kind of trade union involvement varies very widely indeed. Some of the experiments in the United States have taken place in non-union firms, and some trade unionists are concerned that increased satisfaction with the work situation will be used to weaken the allegiance which workers have to their unions. It is a possibility which cannot be excluded.

There can also arise opposition on principle, from a particular kind of Marxist analysis. Delamotte quotes the French Confédération Générale du Travail (CGT) as being suspicious of any development which takes place within a basically capitalist system – 'As long as the capitalistic system exists, organisation of work, whatever forms it takes, will remain subordinate to the goal of maximum profit. . .'(8).

By contrast, the Swedish Trade Union Confederation has made this subject-matter its own and is taking a strong initiating role at the central level in demanding more humane and satisfying jobs for its members, as part of its broader programme of Industrial Democracy. Pending the implementation of the programme, through law and collective bargaining, the initiative at local level is so far generally being taken by companies rather than by local union leaders. The latter are said to be relatively inactive at first, agreeing to experiments but not taking a very positive role. It is in the later stages of experiments, when diffusion and modifications are discussed, that local union leaders are said to find themselves taking an increasing part, their interest and involvement growing, and their own roles changing in the process. One problem mentioned was that, as more and more committees of various kinds are set up locally, the trade union representatives find it more difficult to keep in touch with them.

The Italian Federation of Metal Workers (FIOM–CGIL) has

also integrated this subject-matter into an active union strategy, but in a different way. From their analysis of capitalist society and class conflict, which is no less Marxist than that of the CGT, they have taken the initiative in demanding, within a collective bargaining framework, that alternative solutions should be found to the traditional division of work. The collective agreements concluded in Olivetti and Fiat provide for a reduction in the number of categories of work, the elimination of the lowest categories, and the promotion of workers from lower to higher categories. The Olivetti agreement lists the means which are to be used to make sure that this promotion means not only more money but also changes in work: job re-design with the aim of enlarging and enriching job content, new production methods, successive assignments to different tasks, etc.

In Norway, the Confederation of Norwegian Trade Unions was, from the beginning, one of the partners initiating the Industrial Democracy project. At local level, project committees were always set up to guide the experiments and always included the local shop stewards. Over the years, changes in the membership of project committees have sometimes caused problems; but the researchers report consistently that increased participation by workers in their own work situation has led to increased participation in trade union affairs. In one case, collective bargaining now includes agreements concerning workers' rights to continue learning. This is interpreted to mean the opportunity either of increasing his working experience or of attending certain courses: if this is refused, the matter becomes the subject of formal grievance.

British trade unions have so far adopted a permissive, though rather cautious, attitude. The TUC has joined a tripartite working party which has been set up by the government to look at questions of the quality of working life. It has itself set up a Social Science Working Party, and it has commissioned a study of the effects of one job enrichment programme, particularly the effect on the role of shop stewards. British trade unions have not, so far, initiated or asked for any such programmes themselves, but the wave of productivity bargains which characterised the 1960s included elements of widening job boundaries.

A similarly permissive but slightly guarded attitude is reported from Holland, where the trade unions are said in general to agree to experiments but not to take a very active role in pressing for them.

In all these instances there can be seen a process of working out what congruence there is between the new developments and the structure, history, and thinking of each particular trade union movement.

The organisational context

There are two kinds of organisational pre-conditions, those concerned with the climate of opinion and those concerned with structure.

Climate

The question is often asked whether it is essential for a programme of change to have support from the top of an organisation. It is impossible to generalise about this, but what is essential in any case is support from people who are senior enough to make decisions. It is also essential that there should be some continuity of support. Modern management development programmes often require that managers move from post to post rather often, and this cuts across many kinds of project work. People who have learned to work together need to be allowed to work together long enough for the work to be effective; in any case, no one feels as committed or enthusiastic about a project he inherits as about a project he initiates.

There may be differences, too, between policy statements and actual events. Policy thinking and action relate in various ways in a large organisation, and it is often better to deduce policy from what actually happens than from formal statements. Policy statements from the top give an important impetus, but it is at middle levels, where people have to translate statements into action and deal with the consequences, that the reality is tested.

One important effect of the kind of changes that have been described has been on the role of supervision. There is no doubt that when individual workers or groups of workers become self-regulating, the sheer amount of external control which is exercised over the work process must decrease. What then happens about the roles of supervisors and management can vary. In the Ahmedabad experiments top management withdrew from involvement on the shop floor, and the role of supervision was strengthened, but it was also changed in the direction of managing the boundaries of the system, i.e. its relations with the outside world, rather than controlling what went on inside it. Some supervisors in the new situation speak of themselves as 'human resources managers', i.e. concerned with training and group relations. These two functions, boundary control and the management of human resources, open up important new channels for the development of supervisory roles, and consequently new training needs.

In other situations the number of supervisors, and sometimes the number of levels of supervision, has simply decreased. How this is handled has varied, from carefully planned re-training and re-deployment to a certain callousness – one research worker said: 'Supervisors have been on top for so long, don't ask me to worry about them now'. One British company decided not to go ahead with an experiment when it became clear what the effect would be on their supervisors.

It is no wonder that some foremen's associations are antagonistic to the new developments. Working towards long-term societal goals has to be combined with handling the realities of the present day, and these include the existence of large numbers of real, live, hard-working and probably worried supervisors. It is a new version of the old problem of whether ends justify means, and none the easier for that; but handling it in a creative way which sacrifices neither ends nor means would seem to be a crucial test of adaptive capability. Merely designing Utopias is easy.

Another question frequently asked is whether it is possible to encapsulate the re-design of a job, or whether it must inevitably lead to other changes. Opinions differ on this: while a number of job enrichment exercises turn out to have remained encapsulated, it seems unlikely that one can plan for this to happen. The limits to development tend to be unpredictable; it is an open process. In one organisation, where a group of workers were assembling a piece of equipment under their own control, the department manager was beginning to talk of the need to re-design the accounting system. If the workers were to be responsible for their own accounts, the system would need to be designed for the purpose. Some equipment, too, was turning out to be unsuited to the new method of working and was engaging the ingenuity of the manager.

One thing is asserted with confidence by people who have been involved with such projects: there will at the very least always be consequences for training, and there will always be consequences for payment systems.

The question seems, in any case, the wrong way round. There seems little point in launching on an experiment if it is not congruent with other developments in an organisation. Some minimal steps must be taken at top management level to make it relate to the overall strategy and circumstances of the organisation.

Structure

The need to relate changes in job design to the wider organisational context has been emphasised consistently in this report. Butera, in his account of the experiments at Olivetti, traces how particular economic, technical, and social environments may or may not make these changes possible and how in fact the changes are sometimes enforced by changes of market, technology, or labour force(7).

To summarise a detailed and complex story: during the time leading up to the changes, the market for Olivetti products was becoming more specialised, more demanding in terms of quality needs, and open to stronger competition. This meant that the range of products needed to be widened, each product appeared in an increasing number of models, and the lifetime of the products became shorter. At the same time the rate of change in products was also speeded up by continuous innovation in electronics technology. In manufacturing terms this meant a wider range of different products and models, short product lifetimes, and frequent modifications.

Two different re-organisations of assembly lines have taken place, one into independent sub-assembly units leading to a final assembly, and one into integrated units of thirty people assembling a whole product.

Butera insists that the nature of this new organisation was not merely due to 'organisational imagination', or to labour market factors, morale, or union demands, though all of these played a part. In addition to them, and greatly reinforcing them, there were

A changes in the design of the product, which now consisted of more highly specialised mechanical groups, relatively autonomous from the point of view of function and 'interrupted' by the electronic parts. This made sequential assembly less logical as the mode of production (in turn, if it is desirable to change modes of production, the help of product designers is likely to be needed).

B the market conditions which have been described, which imposed the need for a high degree of flexibility as regards quantity, models mix, and the time scale within which changes were made. In order to achieve such flexibility, they had to avoid re-designing and re-balancing the assembly line every time a variation occurred; and a 'cellular' mode of production, which also involved more highly skilled and flexible people, was much more appropriate, greatly improving the organisation's ability to absorb variances.

However, such solutions are not found automatically: the debate within management on how to improve working life, and also the unions' pressure against alienating work, oriented the research which went into these solutions, accelerating them, defining their details, and supplying the urge and enthusiasm to implement them. The Olivetti case, in fact, shows the complex interaction between structure and climate. The process logic must be in harmony with the logic of product design, *and* there must be people who think this way. Conversely, when people begin to think this way, their product design thinking will be influenced too.

Issues of theory and method

The interpretation and use of concepts

One group of problems stems from the fact that the concepts involved in socio-technical systems theory were formulated at a very high level of generality. The scientists who originally worked with these concepts knew what they were doing, but little has been done to codify this knowledge and make it operationally available. It is easy to agree that the enterprise is an open socio-technical system; it is a little hard to know what to do next, if one's own learning and experience have not been within this tradition. Systems terminology is in any case on the whole very general. At an operational level 'the systems approach' means many different things to different practitioners, who frequently do not define what they take to be the system and what the environment, and which of very many parameters they are tackling. It is an important next task to provide the tools for socio-technical analysis.

In the absence of detailed analytical tools and their spread

76

through training, a number of myths have grown up: for instance, that the answer must always be an autonomous or semi-autonomous group, that any group is better than no group, that work groups are formed by putting people together without regard for their roles and inter-dependencies, that autonomous groups have to be small, etc.

A corollary of the situation where concepts have not been codified and made operational is that no recognisable body of practitioners has been trained, and this has been one of the biggest obstacles to diffusion. When interest is aroused there is no one trained to meet it, all manner of people jump onto the bandwagon, and all manner of odd things may happen.

This brings us into the area of professional training and, even more basically, into the traditional academic disciplines as they are taught in the universities. The practitioners involved in change processes may come from a variety of sources – from engineering, from the social sciences, and (very importantly) from the trade unions. The culture change will not really have taken root, however, until basic engineering training, too, includes the concepts and strategies which are relevant to placing man nearer to the centre of the design process. Economic criteria (which are likewise non-technical) already feature routinely in the training of design engineers. There is no reason why human and social criteria should not feature there in the same way.

In some professional training courses, people like industrial and work study engineers and operational researchers are taught a little about human motivation, and exhorted to take account of the social consequences of what they do; but they are not taught *how* (for instance, how to analyse a role in all its aspects). Therefore, when such practitioners invite the collaboration of social scientists, they usually mean that the social scientist should help sell their project; or they bring him in too late, when the important design options are no longer open. As one research worker put it, 'They say "We'll do it this way, now you go and make the people happy."'

It is also relevant here to mention social science. There is a challenge to the social sciences to get involved in action and not merely in critique. Professional training (as distinct from theoretical teaching and research) is available in applied psychology and for social workers of various kinds. Professional training and the methodology of applied social science are very rarely available for people who work with industrial situations.

In the natural sciences there is clear recognition of a development function, which forms part of the 'research and development' continuum. Some of it is carried out in universities, some in institutions which are half-way between the locales of research and application, and some in the institutions where the research is to be applied – hospitals, industry, etc. In social science the means for financing research generally exist, but the needs of 'development' may not be sufficiently recognised. It means action research and consultancy (not management consultancy, which is something quite different). It is generally a matter not of laboratory experimentation but of working with real problems in real situations, and it raises problems of professional training, of finance, of how to get programmatic rather than piecemeal development, and of the ownership of results.

There is a second set of problems involved in working with socio-technical approaches. These problems have to do with the potential conflict between strategies aimed at finding better solutions and those aimed at enhancing learning; and in consequence with the role of expertise as well.

The idea of joint optimisation of the social and technical sub-systems could be interpreted in the sense that a better state (by implication a 'final' better state) can be defined and reached. This is a static model, which conflicts with the criterion of continuing learning. Optimisation can just as well be seen as a continuing process. The experience of the change is itself part of the situation and changes it, and that is a different model from that of working towards a blueprint. Which one people prefer will depend on their need for security and defined boundaries, which will also influence whether they regard the criteria themselves as rules to be accepted or reviewed.

Most difficult of all, however, is not merely to regard this as a conflict of ideology or personality, but to grasp the idea that both these models are appropriate in different situations. A good strategy is to start with the aim of finding a solution, but with a further aim of then moving towards a learning model. The other way round, of discarding all structure at the outset, can be painful and paralysing. Most confusing of all is the situation where people try, without realising it, to operate both these models simultaneously. It was illustrated by one researcher who said: 'Now they're going to introduce participation by numbers'.

Allied to all this is the question of the role of expertise. In some circles the value attached to self-determination has become so dominant that any form of expertise, too, is rejected as being too authoritarian.*

Some of the current experiments rely on new kinds of knowledge being introduced into design and organisation, while others rely on the growth and creativity involved when people organise and discover things for themselves.

Obviously this is over-simplified, and there is a range of ways of relating to an expert: he may be outside the organisation and visit it occasionally, or work with it continuously for a period; or he may be employed on the staff of the head office and visit plants, almost in the role of an outsider and again with different degrees of involvement; or he may be working directly with an organisation which employs him. His style may involve taking an active part in changes, or he may be available as a resource, holding a watching brief and not intervening or actively refusing to intervene. The issue is also confused by the fact that there are many different kinds of expertise in this area, that experts may not be available, and that experts may turn out to be disappointing.

Among professionals in the field there is a debate about 'designing for' people as distinct from 'designing with' them. A whole range of design strategies is possible, combining elements of 'for' and elements of 'with'. For example, a strategy which is essentially 'designing for' can include phases of feedback and testing-out which involve the people in the situation; or a strategy which is basically 'designing with' can include commissioning an expert to report on existing knowledge or to carry out some experimentation. A great deal in any case depends on the personal integrity and even style of the expert, and on the confidence and trust he manages to earn.

Those who value the process of self-determination in organisation design more highly than the content of the outcome are confronted with a problem of diminishing returns. Those who learn most from the process of design and reorganisation are those who take part in it. But they, too, are designing 'for' someone else, since working groups and populations do not remain static and

* I am indebted to Hans van Beinum for some of this discussion.

79

new members join. Therefore, either the new situation has to be so clearly satisfactory that newcomers will be content to pick up where their predecessors left off; or, on the other hand, review and experimentation and change need to be built into the culture on a continuing basis. It can happen that autonomous work groups become so enthusiastic about what they are doing, and so confident and self-contained, that they have difficulty in absorbing newcomers or relating to the outside world. That becomes the next phase of learning.

Different solutions

Developments in industrial relations are currently proceeding on a number of different lines. These include:

A systems which institutionalise the participation of workers' representatives in decision-making within the enterprise;
B systems concerned with the distribution of wealth and income;
C systems concerned with decision-making in the economy;
D task design and organisation.

It can happen that conflict or competition arises between the proponents of these various lines. This is partly because personal identity and careers become attached to them, partly because people do not have the time or the energy to pursue them all, partly because they fear that attention paid to one may lessen the attention paid to another.

In particular, one of the most important issues to tackle in the immediate future is the relationship between new forms of work organisation and representative systems of participation. It would be very sad if these were to be regarded as alternatives. Increased opportunities for growth and development of the worker at the workplace do not do away with the need to defend collective interests; and representatives will not want to deny opportunities of personal development to their constituents. There are very wide possibilities for integrating the two kinds of development with each other: the patient must not be left to languish while the doctors argue.

Within the framework of work organisation itself, recent experiments fall into two clear types. On the one hand there are those which aim in the first place to make tasks and work roles more intrinsically satisfying. On the other hand a substantial number of experiments have as their starting-point the aim of giving the worker more scope for making decisions, either about matters intrinsically connected with his task, or about matters only partly connected with it. These may reach out into such things as work allocation, production scheduling, and quality control; into personnel policies such as selection and promotion; or still further. Some of these developments then begin to merge into existing or newly devised representative systems.

Where the new work organisation has involved the setting up of autonomous or semi-autonomous work groups, there is a great deal of overlap between the two frames of reference. However, they do not necessarily lead to the same solutions. Re-distributing power, or 'democratisation' of the workplace, and 'humanisation' of the workplace are not necessarily the same thing.

The politics of helping roles

If one is using a systems framework, then the characteristics of helping systems are also relevant to what happens. Those who are in helping roles – industrial engineers, management service people, social scientists, trade unionists – have needs of their own. These needs concern money, training, careers, autonomy, development, the need to make a contribution – in fact all the factors which apply to those who are clients or the subjects of research. If these needs are not catered for openly, they may get repressed and can emerge in some covert form which exploits the client. It is therefore important to be very explicit about the relationship between client and helper and to take great care in working it out.

The pressures of career and development needs among those in helping roles have led to a certain amount of competition between them. This is true in society at large, where property rights to certain problem areas may be disputed; within individual organisations, where the relationship between different service departments may cause problems; or in the development of specific projects. The problem is not so much who has a contribution to make, as who has the right to diagnose. Clients have been known to take advantage of this situation and play helpers off against each other in order to avoid real commitment.

Another set of problems arises from the high value put on innovation and discovery. Reputations are not made from continuing a line of development but from finding or doing something new. Politicians and members of steering groups, as well as people directly involved in research or application, all wish to make a distinctive contribution. This creates scope for continuing innovation, but it may hinder the development and diffusion of that which has already been achieved. It is one reason why there are so many cases and so few programmes.

Something also needs to be said about politics in the other sense. In the Anglo-Saxon countries, 'politics' in social science tend to be about competing schools of thought in theory and method, career pressures with consequent pressures to publish, and the competing claims of different institutions for assignments and research funds. In some continental countries, the alignment of social scientists on party-political lines has become an issue as well.

While hardly anyone claims any longer that social science is value-free, there are differences in the role that personal values play in the work of social scientists. In one tradition, the value judgement is made when one decides whether or not to accept an assignment. After that, the social scientist's task is to help the client organisation clarify its own values, become aware if it is in fact operating within them, and deal with areas of conflict. He can only help in this way if he is accepted by all members of the organisation as being non-partisan. There are other social scientists who openly declare that they are on one side or the other and intend to help that side, or that they are working for some perception of 'society' outside the organisation. These are in fact declarations about who is the client. They are not unprofessional if they are open and if those who are not the client are free to choose whether to collaborate or not.

Another problem has recently arisen around the question of publicity. New forms of work organisation are currently attracting a good deal of public attention and publicity through the media. It is of course vitally important that there should be as widespread information and discussion about these matters as possible. For the people actually involved in the projects, however, publicity can present some rather complex problems. In one organisation, the tactless behaviour of a television crew almost destroyed and certainly inhibited the progress of the experiment.

There are problems for those who are in the public limelight and who may be well aware of the complexities and problems involved in what their organisations are doing but feel compelled to defend it and in the process to simplify it; their constituents back home may sometimes find it difficult to recognise the public descriptions. There are problems for those who are not in the public limelight but who are doing equally interesting and valuable things. There are problems when groups which attract attention come to be regarded, and to regard themselves, as élites. There are problems concerning the time and energy required to deal with visitors. (In one organisation, which had prepared a film about its experiment, the film projectionist complained that he should be paid compensation for the boredom of having to keep running the film!) Publicity, as some organisations are discovering, can be a two-edged sword.

Diffusion

The process of diffusion will no doubt be studied by many people, and few generalisations can as yet be made about it. Diffusion has been rapid and spontaneous in Sweden, and apparently rather slow in Norway. Karlsen's interim report discusses some of the long-term outcomes of the Norwegian experiments, in terms of their wider diffusion within the companies concerned and within Norwegian society:*

1. At Christiania Spigerverk diffusion to other parts of the company is minimal in spite of efforts in 1968 to launch a new experiment in another part of the company. However, in 1970 representatives from one of the mines within the company asked for assistance in analysing their organisation to see whether it would be possible to carry through changes of this type there. The analysis was carried through and its conclusion was that the conditions were good provided some technological changes were made. After this the parties within the mining company themselves took over the experimental work.

2. At Hunsfos the situation now is no longer considered to be 'experimental'. As early as 1969 the parties within the company agreed to making the development programme implicit in the Industrial Democracy project their own, and the process was no longer considered reversible. It has now developed to the point where the local trade union in co-operation with the personnel department are responsible for both carrying through the new

* (27), pp. 154ff.

83

principles of job design in successively new parts of the company, and constructing a completely new training programme for the workers which will give possibilities for significant increases in competence. At the same time they are working on building up a new wage system as support for the training programme. The conclusion is therefore that the internal process of diffusion is solidly embedded in the organisation in the form of a self-sustaining learning process.

3. At Nobø the moving of the panel heater production to Stjørdal meant a significant extension of the frame within which the experimental activities took place. For several reasons: (a) a large increase in the number of people employed from the 50 workers who came from the original experimental area up to the 259 workers now employed in the production, (b) a new and inexperienced management, (c) technological problems in the starting up phase, development has been going on in wave-like motions. In spite of this there seems to be little doubt about it moving in the right direction.

On the other hand diffusion of changes to the main plant at Lade has not taken place.

4. At Norsk Hydro a second experiment in the Magnesium Electrolysis factory began in 1968. Management of the change process has now been taken over by the company itself. On company level the drive to further diffusion of the change process seems to have been minimal for some years. It is important to remember that Norsk Hydro is the largest company in Norway and as a result of its size has a well-developed bureaucracy which in itself is not easily changed. On the other hand a good deal of activity at top level during the last year may indicate that there has been a necessary period of latency. The ideas from the ID project are now fully accepted by both parties as company policy, even if the gap between policy statements and concrete actions can be great within large companies.

At industry and national level, the diffusion of ideas has been substantial, but the development of further work has not been as rapid as the researchers would have wished. One reason may be that a new generation has revived emphasis on representative forms of democracy. Another reason, suggested by Karlsen, is that the development of centralised electronic data processing systems has been an inhibiting factor in diffusion, since managements have been afraid that they might be losing out in competitive terms if they did not go along with such logical developments. The situation is reminiscent of the supervisors in Ahmedabad, and the foreman who had to 'hold himself back' from taking an apparently obvious logical step. The decision about which direction to pursue arises not once, at the beginning of an experiment or programme, but at many points along the way.

Policy-making as a learning process

The first generation of problems has been about finding ways to humanise the nature of work and testing these in practice. The next generation of problems is about building these ideas more solidly into the industrial and social fabric, and about relating different developments in industrial relations to each other.

How to do this must itself be regarded as a learning process. Western industrial society is in a learning phase, and it is a rather disjointed one. Developments in the countries visited have been very different. In the U.K. some major early theoretical developments were followed by rather few practical experiences, and some of these have been carried out in the context of client–consultant relationships, with important studies not published. At the level of public policy a tripartite steering committee has only very recently been set up by the Government and has not yet formulated its plans. In Holland, probably the main single influence has been the existence of a substantial number of highly trained social scientists. There is post-graduate training available in the skills of consultancy and action roles; and the contribution of social scientists to social action, including their employment in industry, is well established and accepted. Developments in Norway have been briefly described. In Sweden, developments have been recent and rapid and, although there are a lot of social scientists in Sweden too, many of these experiments do not involve the use of social scientists. Diffusion has been through the employer network, through the active involvement of the central trade union organisations, and through party political action.

There are big time-lags and differences

A in the evolution of norms and values, and the institutions which embody them;

85

B in the development and spread of the relevant methods and concepts;

C even in the development of simple efficiency. (While some organisations have reached economic levels where they are wondering in which directions to develop next, others are still struggling with an earlier generation of problems. It has to be remembered that inefficient organisations – where 'they can't even get the invoices out on time' – are also very frustrating to work in.)

An important factor in this disjointedness is the discrepancy between the speed of change and the speed of communication. An experiment of this kind develops slowly, as anyone knows who has taken part in one. Information, on the other hand, travels fast: no sooner does a company announce plans for re-organisation, than plane-loads of visitors from all over the world flock in to take a look.

Looking back at the industrial democracy project in Norway, Thorsrud and Herbst describe the various institutions that evolved in terms of policy-making as a learning process(44). It is a basic concept, and it means that the institutions themselves cannot be copied. Both for organisations and societies it is inviting the risk of costly and time-consuming error to copy patterns and forms which were evolved in other circumstances. Other people's solutions are the result of their experience; this cannot be transferred, though it can spread through working with them. Therefore, while knowledge, ideas, and suggestions can be gleaned from other people's experience, solutions have in the end to be worked out for oneself.

For individual organisations, this means that the question is not how to introduce autonomous work groups. The question is what organisational forms can be evolved that are appropriate both to the tasks and to the value systems of the organisation, in the light of economic goals and goals involving human development. This may involve a great deal of work in eliciting what the tasks and the value system actually are.

At societal level, some of the relevant questions are:

1. *What are the pressures for change?* Basically this implies examining concepts of efficiency.* Change is only likely to be successful if it arises from a felt need and not from a wish to copy fashion. Such

* For a discussion of the social role of production management, see (26).

a need may be experienced through problems of adapting to changing markets and technologies or through finding that the labour market has changed.

The need for change may also arise from felt discrepancies between industrial and other value systems in society. What is the relationship between industry and opinion leaders in other fields? How do people in industry feel about it? Are there incompatibilities between the expectations engendered by the education system and the realities of the world of work? How do they express themselves?

It is an important debate, but it is also important not to conduct it in a coercive manner. It is extremely difficult to say that one is opposed to something that calls itself 'the quality of working life' or 'organisational development'. If people are not allowed to express their real views, then penalties will accrue later, when reality eventually breaks through.

2. *If there is a wish for change, what kind of change?* Here it is necessary to consider new forms of work organisation in the light of other changes. All over Europe there is currently a spate of legislation and proposals for various forms of increased participation. Changes concerning the nature of work itself must somehow find a place in all this, without damaging either representation or bargaining.

3. *What resources exist or need to be provided?* These are questions about the institutions of research, training, and higher education: they include questions about the traditional division of knowledge into self-contained disciplines and faculties. When people of high calibre – from whatever background – are asked to apply themselves to industrial problems, they must be enabled, without loss of professional status, to work in a problem-centred rather than a discipline-centred way. This may require the design of new institutions.

4. *Finally, there is the question of the role of government.* Countries vary greatly in the degree to which they look to central government to regulate working arrangements. Legislation about this kind of subject-matter is difficult to formulate and may not be desirable. However, Appendix 2 provides a number of ideas for ways in which government could support these developments.

Appendix 1. Extracts from *Scientific Management and Labor* by R. F. Hoxie

In pursuing this study, the investigator and the official experts were governed throughout by two standards of judgment.

First, scientific management, in its relations to labor, must be judged...mainly by what it proves to be in its actual operation ...Scientific management, in this respect, is like any other thing in the social or material world. It is what it is in fact, and not what the ideals or theories of its advocates or opponents would have it to be...Like all other things which affect humanity, it must, therefore, be judged by actual results and tendencies.

Secondly, it follows that the scope of scientific management... is to be determined...by what is found to exist and persist in the systematized portions of shops designated to represent it...

Throughout the study here presented, therefore, scientific management must be understood to mean the systems created and applied by Mr Taylor, Mr Gantt, and Mr Emerson, and their adherents, as these systems actually work out in the shops designated by them...

The claims of scientific management relative to labor

[Hoxie mentions the various leaders and would-be leaders who have arisen, each with his own doctrine, and goes on to say that 'the Taylor system has been and still is regarded in most quarters as scientific management par excellence and practically identified with the more inclusive term'.

The 'general spirit and character' of 'the labor claims of scientific management' may be indicated by the following statements.]

1. *The general definition of scientific management.* Scientific management is a system devised by industrial engineers for the purpose of subserving the common interests of employers,

workmen, and society at large, through the elimination of avoidable wastes, the general improvement of the processes and methods of production, and the just and scientific distribution of the product.

2. *Fundamental principles of scientific management.* Scientific management rests on the fundamental economic principles that harmony of interests exists between employers and workers, and that high general wages and better general conditions of employment can be secured through low labor cost.

3. *The relation of scientific management to fact and law.* Scientific management attempts to substitute in the relations between employers and workers the government of fact and law for the rule of force and opinion. It substitutes exact knowledge for guesswork and seeks to establish a code of natural laws equally binding upon employers and workmen.

4. *The scientific and democratic character of scientific management.* Scientific management is thus at once scientific and democratic.

In time and motion study it has discovered and developed an accurate scientific method by which the great mass of laws governing the easiest and most productive movements of men are registered...

It pays men rather than positions and...makes possible the rewarding of each workman on the basis of his efficiency. It makes possible the scientific selection of workmen...

It analyzes the operations of industry into their natural parts, makes careful studies of fatigue and sets the task on the basis of a large number of performances by men of different capacities and with due and scientific allowance for the human factor and legitimate delays.

It assigns to each workman a definite and by him accomplishable task, institutes rational rest periods,... eliminates pace setters, standardizes performance, and guards the workers against over-speeding and exhaustion...

It substitutes the rule of law for the arbitrary decisions of foremen, employers, and unions...

Scientific management thus democratizes industry. It gives a voice to both parties and substitutes joint obedience of employers and workers to fact and law for obedience to personal authority ...It gives the worker in the end equal voice with the employer; both can refer only to the arbitrament of science and fact.

[After outlining scientific management claims concerning productive efficiency and labour welfare, Hoxie goes on to describe how both Gantt and Emerson would modify the claims made by Taylor upon all points. Emerson's attitude is that 'We have no system. What we attempt to do is to apply certain principles. We are willing to adopt any methods, any device, if it is advantageous.']

The trade union objections to scientific management

1. *The general definition of scientific management.* Organized labor understands by the term, 'scientific management', certain well-defined 'efficiency systems' which have been recently devised by individuals and small groups under the leadership and in imitation of men like Frederick W. Taylor, H. L. Gantt and Harrington Emerson... Organized labor makes a clear distinction between 'scientific management' thus defined and 'science in management'...

2. *Scientific management in its relation to labor welfare.* 'Scientific management' thus defined is a device employed for the purpose of increasing production and profits; and tends to eliminate consideration for the character, rights and welfare of the employees...

In spirit and essence, it is a cunningly devised speeding-up and sweating system...

It intensifies the modern tendency towards specialization of the work and the task...

It displaces day work and day wage by task work and the piece-rate, premium and bonus systems of payment.

It tends to set the task on the basis of 'stunt' records of the strongest and swiftest workers without due allowance for human element or legitimate delays... which usually result in giving the worker less than the regular rate of pay for his extra exertion...

It establishes a rigid standard of wages regardless of the progressive increase in the cost of living...

It tends to lengthen the hours of labor; shortens the tenure of service; lessens the certainty and continuity of employment; and leads to over-production and the increase of unemployment.

It condemns the worker to a monotonous routine...

It puts into the hands of employers at large an immense mass of information and methods which may be used unscrupulously to the detriment of the workers...

3. *Scientific management in its relation to industrial democracy.* 'Scientific management' is undemocratic; it is a reversion to industrial autocracy...

It tends to gather up and transfer to the management all the traditional knowledge, the judgment and the skill of the workers...

It allows the workman ordinarily no voice in hiring or discharge...

It greatly intensifies unnecessary managerial dictation and discipline...

It introduces the spirit of mutual suspicion and contest among the men...

It has refused to deal with the workers except as individuals.

It is incompatible with and destructive of unionism;... [and] of collective bargaining.

4. *The unscientific character of scientific management.* 'Scientific management'... does not take all the elements into consideration but deals with human beings as it does with inanimate machines.

... [It ignores] habits, temperament, and traditions of work and tends to minimize the acquired skill of the workers.

It greatly increases the number of 'unproductive workers'...

It is unscientific and unfair in its determination of the task...

It is based on the principle of the survival of the fittest and tends to disregard the physical welfare of the workers.

5. *The inefficiency of scientific management.* 'Scientific management'... does not tend to develop general and long-time economic efficiency.

It tends to emphasize quantity of product at the expense of quality...

It is incapable of extensive application...

6. *Scientific management and industrial unrest.* 'Scientific management' intensifies the conditions of industrial unrest.

It libels the character of the workmen, and its methods are evidence of suspicion and direct question of the honesty and fairness of the workers.

It... is regarded by [the workers] with extreme distaste.

It pits workman against workman...

It increases the points of friction and offers no guarantee against industrial warfare and is conducive to strikes.

91

Critical examination of scientific management in its relations to labor

...At its best, as set forth by Mr Taylor, and as realized in practice, scientific management means a thoroughgoing improvement and standardization of the material equipment and productive organization of the plant before an attempt is made to apply its peculiar methods and devices to the determination of standards of labor efficiency and wage payments...

Scientific management not only holds out, therefore, possibilities of substantial benefits to labor, but it points the way and the only way toward raising the standard of living for all classes of labor and for society at large...

If scientific management be shown to have positive objectionable features, both from the standpoint of labor and the welfare of society, this...calls...for intelligent social action to eliminate that which is detrimental and to supplement and control that which is beneficial to all. Fortunately, scientific management, in spite of dogmatic statements of certain leaders, is not one rigid and indivisible whole which must be accepted or rejected as it is...

Scientific management in practice

...In the course of the present investigation, no single shop was found which could be said to represent fully and faithfully the Taylor system as presented in the treatise on 'Shop Management'; no representative of the Gantt system was encountered, complete and unmixed with alien elements; no shop was discovered wherein the Emerson ideals were completely demonstrated and held full sway, and no two shops were found in which identically or even approximately the same policies and methods were established and adhered to throughout...

The best ideals of scientific management...require that the installation of the system shall begin with a thoroughgoing study, improvement where possible, and standardization of the material equipment, managerial organization and productive processes of the shop...

Notwithstanding, however, the position taken by the authorities in this matter..., in practice there is no general adherence to the order of installation as laid down by Mr Taylor, and, in many cases, there is a notable neglect of the process of organic and material improvement. The better class of experts do indeed insist on beginning the installation. . . with the study and standardization of the material and organic factors. But. . . they are not able to carry this work forward [because] the management usually wants to see quicker results. . . The better class in this respect are decidedly in a minority. It is safe to say that most of those who offer their services to employers have not themselves the ability or the willingness to install scientific management in accordance with the Taylor formula and ideals. . .

It must be conceded that, generally speaking, the workers in scientific management shops seem to be a select class *when compared with the same classes of workers outside*, but this result appears to be due not so much to the method of initial selection employed as to subsequent events which tend to weed out the less satisfactory material. It certainly is not the outcome of any unique or scientific discoveries and achievements in connection with the process of hiring. . .

Nowhere did the writer discover any scientific or adequate methods employed for adapting the worker to the task, that is, for 'setting each man to the highest task for which his physical and intellectual capacity fits him'. . .

It is just in this connection, however [Taylor's claim that time and motion study is 'the accurate scientific method' of setting times], that the unbiased investigator receives perhaps his strongest impressions of the diversities of the so-called scientific management methods. Far from being the invariable and purely objective matters that they are pictured, the methods and results of time study and task setting are, in practice, the special sport of individual judgment and opinion, subject to all the possibilities of diversity, inaccuracy and injustice that arise from human ignorance and prejudice. . .

There are two main purposes for which time study may be employed. It may be used primarily for the study, improvement, and standardization of the methods of doing the work under observation. . . or it may have for its main or sole purpose the fixing of a definite task time or efficiency scale. . .

Great possibilities of advantage both to the employer and the workmen exist in time study employed for the purpose first named. . .

Unfortunately, scientific management employers, in general, do not live up to the highest ideals in this connection. Some, even, do not recognize this vital distinction between time study for standardization and time study for task setting or efficiency rating. The result is that in a large proportion of the shops time study for standardization is relatively neglected...

More noticeable by far are the variations in the actual methods employed in determining the time allowed for the accomplishment of tasks or for the rating of efficiency, and especially the part which fallible human judgment and individual prejudice may and do play in arriving thus at what are assumed to be objective scientific results...

In the present case, the assumed objective scientific fact is the time allowed the workers for doing a definite task. It is claimed to be a scientific fact in that it is an accurate scientific demonstration of what the workers can accomplish without over-strain and exhaustion. But in order to uphold this claim it is evident that the judgment of the time study man must not enter into the process of its determination in such a way as to affect the fact itself... His function must be purely that of discovery...

At a score of points in this process, the judgment of the employer, the time study man or the workers may be exercised so as to produce variation that will affect and alter the task itself. In other words, the time study process includes a score of factors variable with the judgment and will of those immediately concerned, variation in any or all of which acts as a determinant of the task. [Hoxie then goes on to list seventeen factors which may vary, subject to human will.]

1 The general attitude, ideals and purposes of the management and the consequent general instructions given to the time study man;
2 The character, intelligence, training and ideals of the time study man;
3 The degree to which the job to be timed and all its appurtenances have been studied and standardized looking to uniform conditions in its performance for all the workers;
4 The amount of change thus made from old methods and conditions of performance, e.g., the order of performance, the motions eliminated, and the degree of habituation of the

workers to the old and the new situation when the task is set;

5 The mode of selection of the workers to be timed and their speed and skill relative to the other members of the group;

6 The relative number of workers timed and the number of readings considered sufficient to secure the result desired;

7 The atmospheric conditions, time of day, time of year, the mental and physical condition of the workers when timed and the judgment exercised in reducing these matters to the 'normal';

8 The character and amount of special instruction and special training given the selected workers before timing them;

9 The instructions given to them by the time study man as to care and speed, etc., to be maintained during the timing process;

10 The attitude of the time study man toward the workers being timed and the secret motives and aims of the workers themselves;

11 The judgment of the time study man as to the pace maintained under timing relative to the 'proper', 'normal' or maximum speed which should be demanded;

12 The checks on the actual results used by the time study man in this connection;

13 The method and mechanism used for observing and recording times and the degree of accuracy with which actual results are caught and put down;

14 The judgment exercised by the time study man in respect to the retention or elimination of possibly inaccurate or 'abnormally' high or low readings;

15 The method used in summing up the elementary readings to get the 'necessary' elementary time;

16 The method employed in determining how much should be added to the 'necessary time' as a human allowance;

17 The method of determining the 'machine allowance'...

If space permitted, each one of the seventeen points enumerated above could be considered, and it could be shown in each case that judgment enters not only into determining the method pursued but as a determinant of the task time set...

The demonstration, however, of the unscientific character of time study and task setting does not at all prove that the method is necessarily impracticable or unjust to the workers. On the contrary, if the management is honestly seeking the best good of all concerned, and if the time study man is well trained, experienced, with good analytical ability, good judgment, and tact, there can be no question that time study promises much more equitable results than can be secured by the ordinary methods . . .

But it must not be forgotten that great knowledge creates also greater opportunities for the unscrupulous and that a method, which in benevolent and intelligent hands makes better dealing possible, may be woefully abused by the ignorant and unscrupulous, and observation proves that time study for task setting is no exception to the rule . . .

In fact, the time study man, who, if scientific management is to make good the most important of its labor claims, should be among the most highly trained and influential officials in the shop, a scientist in viewpoint, a wise arbiter between employer and workmen, is, in general, a petty functionary, a specialist workman, a sort of clerk, who has no voice in the counsels of the higher officials . . .

So long, therefore, as industry continues to be the complex and diversified thing that it is, including in its range unskilled, routine and repetitive operations and work which requires on the job the highest exercise of manual skill and judgment, so long as it is in flux, developing continuously new products, new modes, new machinery and processes, and so long as productive concerns are required in order to survive, to adapt themselves quickly to fluctuating market demands, this element of economy will without doubt continue to operate in a way to limit the legitimate scope of time study and task setting and will retard the uniform development of ideals and technique in this connection . . .

With such possibilities in view, neither in the present nor in the near future is there any reasonable ground for the sweeping labor claims of scientific management based on time study as a method of task setting and efficiency rating.

[Hoxie then describes in detail the various 'systems of payment devised by the leaders of the schools of scientific management under consideration'.] None of them, except the differential piece rate, makes it clear that scientific management intends to purchase labor by specification. All of them definitely belie the claim that scientific management pays workers in exact proportion to their efficiency...

Finally, all of the systems tend in their direct effects to center the attention of the worker on his individual interest and gain and to repress the development of group consciousness and interest...

The almost universal declaration of scientific management experts and shop managers is that rates once established are never altered...Nevertheless, to say that rates under scientific management are never cut and to assume that the whole influence of scientific management is in the direction of maintenance of rates would be patently opposed to the facts. Rates are rarely, if ever, cut openly in scientific management shops, but the payment methods employed, together with the methods of setting tasks, lend themselves readily to indirect cutting, and there is no doubt that what is openly decried is sometimes accomplished by indirection...

Mr Taylor conceives of the industrial situation as one in which the relations between employers and workers are governed by a fundamental harmony of interests. This being assumed, perfect equality between them and complete democracy in all their relationships is to be sought in sweeping aside the personal authority of the employer and the arbitrary rules and regulations of the workmen with all the machinery for negotiations and the enforcement of decisions created by both, and substituting in all matters the impersonal dictates of natural law and fact...

The trade unionists, on the other hand, conceive of the industrial situation as one in which the interests of the employers and workmen are fundamentally opposed, at least as concerns the division of the product and the conditions of work that relate themselves closely to this...

[Hoxie goes on to say that in general two classes of manager were to be found, those who shared Taylor's belief in harmony of interests, and those who, to all intents and purposes, took the trade union view; but he claims that even most of those 'who expressed belief in the ideals of harmony and in the democratic principle were far from being willing to go the whole route and put into practice the democratic deductions of the Taylor concept ...in the end, it was generally found that the democracy of these men had a string attached to it...In short, the democracy of this sort of scientific managers usually turned out to be on analysis a species of benevolent despotism. . . .' He then develops the argument that scientific management tends to emphasise the individual and, in practice, 'to weaken the power of the individual worker as against the employer'.]

The writer has in mind one of the best shops where the management is thoroughly fair and liberal in spirit, in which conditions existed which would not be tolerated for a moment by a body of workers with a real voice in affairs, or by the management if it knew of them, yet the front office here is always open. The fact is that where workers are individualized as in scientific management shops, their just complaints will not ordinarily be voiced even to a management in which they have confidence, much less to an autocratic employer. Anyone who knows anything of working-class psychology understands perfectly well that the individual worker does not dare to unburden himself to his superiors even under the best of circumstances. . . Time after time the writer was informed that the workers were entirely satisfied because no complaints had been made for months or only one a month or year. . .

At the outset of his investigation the attention of the writer was forcibly called to certain cases where unionism was tolerated in scientific measurement shops, as proof of the tolerant attitude of the managers, and the entire compatibility of scientific management and unionism. Investigation proved that inferences drawn from such cases were, in general, altogether misleading. . . In one case, particularly, where assurance had been given that perfect harmony existed between the management and the organized employees, the superintendent was quizzed in regard to the functions and activities of the union. About these things he was absolutely uninformed; why the union existed or what it did, he could not tell. He had no dealings with it as such, and the men who belonged to it were treated in no way differently from the other individual workers in the shop.

Before [certain great benefits which might derive from the movement, and the curing of many of its shortcomings] can be brought about, however, certain potent causes of present evil must be eradicated. The first of these is a persistent attempt on the part of experts and managers to apply scientific management and its methods. . .indiscriminately and arbitrarily to all sorts of industries, under all sorts of conditions and to all kinds of work.

For this, Mr Taylor is to be held largely responsible. His experience primarily was that of a machinist. He worked out a system of control for application to the machine shop where the dangers of overspeeding and overfatigue are not as great as in some other industries and the human factor requires relatively less consideration in the setting of the task. But, being an enthusiast, he proceeded at once to broad generalizations, based on his machine shop experience. He believed that he had discovered industrial laws and methods of universal applicability. And being also an idealist, he failed to distinguish between what might be and what is...

A second chief source of danger and evil to labor in the application of scientific management is that it offers its wares in the open market, but it has developed no means by which it can control the use of these by the purchaser...

Scientific management as a movement is cursed with fakirs... The way is open to all. No standards or requirements, private or public, have been developed by the application of which the goats can be separated from the sheep...Almost anyone can show the average manufacturing concern where it can make some improvements in its methods. So the scientific management shingles have gone up all over the country, the fakirs have gone into the shops, and in the name of scientific management have reaped temporary gains to the detriment of the real article, the employers and the workers...

Fake scientific management experts, however, are not alone responsible for the...diversity and immaturity of scientific management in practice...The fact is that, on the whole and barring some notable exceptions, the sponsors and adherents of scientific management – experts and employers alike – are profoundly ignorant of very much that concerns the broader humanitarian and social problems which it creates and involves, especially as these touch the character and welfare of labor... The prominent members of the scientific management group – engineers and employers for the most part – seem to be developing their economic and social theories, in fact, almost wholly on the basis of their own experience and of the simple, fundamental and general assumptions which economists and social scientists generally have tried out and abandoned...

This naïve ignorance of social science and of the social effects of scientific management, and the cocksureness which accompanies it are perhaps the most potent cause of the diversity and immaturity of scientific management where it touches the welfare of the labor group. It is because of this ignorance and unwarranted assurance that there is a strong tendency on the part of scientific management experts to look upon the labor end of their work as the least difficult and requiring the least careful consideration. . .

The crude and variable handling of the labor end of the scientific management installation and operation is a natural consequence. It is largely for this reason that scientific management experts who have had actual experience in only one line of industry boldly undertake the systematization of shops in industries with which they are practically unfamiliar. The affair in their mind is simply productive efficiency through the application of certain mechanical and organic principles. . .

In the meanwhile, we need more thorough study and general publicity concerning the true character, policies, and methods of scientific management, its possibilities, responsibilities and limitations; concerning the real character, intelligence and spirit of those engaged in its application, the qualities and qualifications required by the best social standards for the exercise of this power and responsibility, and the progressive education of scientific management experts and employers, labor and the public, to the needs and requirements of the situation.

Appendix 2. Some policy suggestions

The following are some tentative suggestions for ways in which government might support the development of new forms of work organisation. They are designed to cope with a number of dilemmas, which arise because:

A one cannot be sure about economic risks, and this may inhibit inventiveness;

B it is hard to know how to move from isolated experiments to critical mass and a change in trend;

C it is hard to know what part can be played by government and legislation; and at the same time,

D while initiatives are left to individual firms, the unions are uncertain about the motives behind them and about their own part in controlling them.

Protected experiment scheme

When the management and workers' representatives in an organisation agree on the outlines of an experiment or project, they would first submit their plans for inclusion in the scheme. All the plans proposed would be vetted by an independent body (possibly consisting of employer and union representatives and academics). Criteria would have to be worked out by this body but might, for instance, include such things as the technical feasibility of the proposals, the role given in the projects to union representation, and the willingness to evaluate and publish results.

Once admitted to the scheme, organisations would become eligible for two kinds of support:

A Direct support could take many forms but might, for instance, include training allowances for an initial period, start-up allowances, machinery and equipment grants, or tax allowances.

B It might be possible to devise a form of insurance on which organisations in the scheme could draw if their projects ran them into serious difficulties and losses.

This structure is designed to be flexible, leaving the actual scale of resources to policy decision. The scheme can admit one experiment per year, on a competitive basis, or three, or twenty, or all those that meet the criteria set down. The insurance fund, too, could be either finite or renewable.

The design of new technologies

In the design of new technologies it is not out of the question to think of legislation. This suggestion has already been referred to in the text: it might be possible to make it mandatory to devote a percentage of new capital investment, or a specified sum per work-role envisaged, to design and development activities which are concerned with the tasks and work-roles being created. In order to encourage diversity and creativity, the nature of these activities need not be specified. Some of the direct support benefits described above might also be made available.

References

(1) Agersnap, F., J. Finn, and P. Duus. 'New Forms of Co-operation'. Duplicated report, Institute of Organisation and Industrial Sociology, Copenhagen.

(2) Agervold, M. 'Swedish Experiments in Democracy', in A. B. Cherns and L. E. Davis (eds.), *The Quality of Working Life*. New York: Free Press, 1975.

(3) Banbury, J. 'Optimality and Information System Design', paper read at International Research Conference on Operational Research, Chester, 1973.

(4) Blake, R. R., and Jane S. Mouton. *The Managerial Grid*. Houston, Texas: Gulf Publishing Co., 1964.

(5) Brown, W. *Exploration in Management*. London: Heinemann, 1960.

(6) Burns, T., and G. Stalker. *The Management of Innovation*. London: Tavistock, 1961.

(7) Butera, F. 'Contribution to the Analysis of Structural Variables Affecting Emerging Patterns of Job Design: The Olivetti Case', in A. B. Cherns and L. E. Davis (eds.), *The Quality of Working Life*. New York: Free Press, 1975.

(8) Confédération Générale du Travail. 'Pour des conditions de travail plus humaines en rapport avec notre temps: positions et propositions de la CGT' (cited in (12) below).

(9) Cox, D., and K. M. Dyce Sharp. 'Research on the Unit of Work', *Occupational Psychology*, 25 (1951), 90.

(10) Dalziel, S. J., and Lisl Klein. 'The Case of Pakitt Ltd'. Duplicated report, Warren Spring Laboratory of Department of Scientific and Industrial Research (now Ministry of Technology), 1960.

(11) Davis, L. E., R. R. Canter, and J. Hoffman. 'Current Job Design Criteria', *Journal of Industrial Engineering*, 6 (1955), 5–11.

(12) Delamotte, Y. 'Union Attitudes to Quality of Working

Life', in A. B. Cherns and L. E. Davis (eds.), *The Quality of Working Life*. New York: Free Press, 1975.

(13) Emery, F. E. 'Characteristics of Socio-technical Systems'. Tavistock Institute of Human Relations, Document no. 527, 1959.

(14) Emery, F. E. 'The Democratisation of the Workplace', *Manpower and Applied Psychology*, 1 (1967), 118–29.

(15) Emery, F. E., and E. Thorsrud. *Form and Content in Industrial Democracy*. London: Tavistock, 1969.

(16) Freud, S. *Civilization and its Discontents*, in James Strachey *et al.* (eds.), *Standard Edition of the Complete Works of Sigmund Freud*, vol. 21. London: Hogarth Press and Institute of Psychoanalysis, 1961, pp. 64–145.

(17) Goldthorpe, J. H., D. Lockwood, F. Bechhofer, and J. Platt. *The Affluent Worker*. Cambridge: University Press, 1968.

(18) Harding, D. W. 'A Note on the Subdivision of Assembly Work', *Journal of the National Institute of Industrial Psychology*, 5 (1931), 261–4.

(19) Hedberg, M. 'Summary of Trial Activities at present being conducted concerning Changes in Work Organisation'. Duplicated report, Swedish Council for Personnel Administration, Stockholm, 1972.

(20) Herbst, P. G. *Socio-technical Design*. London: Tavistock, 1974.

(21) Herzberg, F., B. Mausner, and B. B. Snyderman. *The Motivation to Work*. New York: Wiley, 1959.

(22) Higgin, G. *Symptoms of Tomorrow*. London: Ward Lock/Plume Press, 1973.

(23) Hoxie, R. F. *Scientific Management and Labor*. New York: D. Appleton, 1915.

(24) Hulin, C. L., and M. R. Blood. 'Job Enlargement, Individual Differences and Worker Responses', *Psychological Bulletin*, 69 (1968), 41–55.

(25) Jahoda, Marie. 'Notes on Work', in R. Loewenstein, L. Newman, M. Schur, and A. Solnit (eds.), *Psychoanalysis: A General Psychology*. New York: International University Press, 1966, 622–33.

(26) Johansson, S. B. 'On the Need of New Concepts for Production Management', paper read at 2nd International Conference on Production Research,

Technical University of Denmark, August 1973.

(27) Karlsen, J. I. 'A Monograph on the Norwegian Industrial Democracy Project'. Work Research Institutes (Oslo), Document no. 15/1972.

(28) King, D. 'Vocational Training in View of Technical Change'. E.P.A. Project no. 418, March 1960.

(29) Klein, Lisl. *The Meaning of Work*. Tract no. 349. London: Fabian Society, 1963.

(30) Klein, Lisl. *Multiproducts Ltd*. London: H.M.S.O., 1964.

(31) Klein, Lisl. *A Social Scientist in Industry*. London: Gower Press, 1976.

(32) Lawrence, P. R., and J. W. Lorsch. *Organization and Environment: Managing Differentiation and Integration*. Cambridge, Mass.: Harvard University Press, 1967.

(33) Likert, R. *New Patterns of Management*. New York: McGraw-Hill, 1961.

(34) Lupton, T. *On the Shop Floor*. Oxford: Pergamon, 1963.

(35) McGregor, D. *The Human Side of Enterprise*. New York: McGraw-Hill, 1960.

(36) Murray, H. 'An Introduction to Socio-technical Systems at the Level of the Primary Work Group'. Tavistock Institute of Human Relations, Document no. HRC 492, 1970.

(37) Neff, W. S. 'Psychoanalytic Conceptions of the Meaning of Work', *Psychiatry*, 28 (1965), 324–33.

(38) Pugh, D. S., D. J. Hickson, C. R. Hinings, and C. Turner. 'The Context of Organisational Structures', *Administrative Science Quarterly*, 14 (1969), 91–114.

(39) Rice, A. K. *Productivity and Social Organization: The Ahmedabad Experiment*. London: Tavistock, 1958.

(40) Roethlisberger, F. J., and W. J. Dickson. *Management and the Worker*. Cambridge, Mass.: Harvard University Press, 1939.

(41) Shackel, B., and Lisl Klein. 'Refuelling at London Airport', *Applied Ergonomics*, forthcoming.

(42) Swedish Trade Union Confederation. 'Industrial Democracy', programme adopted by the 1971 Conference. Stockholm, 1972.

(43) Taylor, F. W. *The Principles of Scientific Management*. New York: Harper & Row, 1911.

(44) Thorsrud, E. 'Policy-making as a Learning Process' in A. B. Cherns, R. Sinclair, and W. I. Jenkins (eds.), *Social Science and Government: Policies and Problems*. London: Tavistock, 1972.

(45) Trist, E. L., and K. W. Bamforth. 'Some Social and Psychological Consequences of the Longwall Method of Coal Getting', *Human Relations*, 4 (1951), 3–38.

(46) Trist, E. L., G. W. Higgin, H. Murray, and A. B. Pollock. *Organisational Choice*. London: Tavistock, 1963.

(47) Turner, A. N., and P. R. Lawrence. *Industrial Jobs and the Worker*. Cambridge, Mass.: Harvard University Graduate School of Business Administration, 1965.

(48) Vernon, H. M., S. Wyatt, and A. D. Ogden. 'On the Extent and Effects of Variety in Repetitive Work', Industrial Fatigue Research Board, Report no. 26. London: H.M.S.O., 1924.

(49) Wilkinson, A. *A Survey of Some Western European Experiments in Motivation*. London: Institute of Work Study Practitioners, 1970.

(50) Wilson, N. A. B. 'On the Quality of Working Life', Department of Employment, Manpower Paper no. 7. London: H.M.S.O., 1973.

(51) Woodward, Joan. *Industrial Organisation: Theory and Practice*. Oxford: University Press, 1965.

(52) Woodward, Joan (ed.). *Industrial Organisation: Behaviour and Control*. Oxford: University Press, 1970.

(53) *Work in America*. Report of a Special Task Force to the Secretary of Health, Education and Welfare. Cambridge, Mass.: MIT Press, [1972].

(54) Wyatt, S., and J. A. Fraser, assisted by F. G. L. Stock. 'The Comparative Effects of Variety and Uniformity in Work', Industrial Fatigue Research Board, Report no. 52. London: H.M.S.O., 1928.